A LIVING LEGACY

A Fortnight in the Forge

Vivien Firth

Copyright © 2023 by Vivien Firth

The right of Vivien Firth to be identified as the author of this work has been asserted by her in accordance with the Copyright, Designs and Patents Act 1988.

All right reserved.
No Part of this publication may be reproduced or transmitted in any form or by any means, electronic or mechanical, including photocopying, recording, or any information storage and retrieval system, without prior permission in writing of the author.

Scriptures taken from the Holy Bible, New International Version®, NIV®. Copyright © 1973, 1978, 1984, 2011 by Biblica, Inc.™ Used by permission of Zondervan. All rights reserved worldwide.

Scripture taken from the New King James Version®. Copyright © 1982 by Thomas Nelson. Used by permission. All rights reserved.

Scripture quotations marked (CEV) are from the Contemporary English Version Copyright © 1991, 1992, 1995 by American Bible Society. Used by Permission.

Scripture quotations marked (NLT) are taken from the Holy Bible, New Living Translation, copyright ©1996, 2004, 2015 by Tyndale House Foundation. Used by permission of Tyndale House Publishers, Carol Stream, Illinois 60188. All rights reserved.

A LIVING LEGACY
written to give honour to :-

THE JESUS CHRIST, WHO BY HIS GRACE,
FORGES US IN THE FIRE OF HIS
ALL-CONSUMING LOVE,
TO IGNITE HOPE
AND ESTABLISH TRUTH
IN THE HEART OF HIS PEOPLE AND NATIONS

FORGED FOREVER ONE
AT THE FOOT OF THE CROSS

Acknowledgments

I thank God for His faithful servants Kyoo Dae and Bridget Lee, who were prepared to lay all on the altar that this vision could be birthed. Their faithful prayers sown into the land and legacy left from the time of Rees Howells Intercessor, have helped new generations be raised up through, worship intercession and mission. Their pioneer work and selfless- dedication has left a living legacy in many hearts throughout the world and I acknowledge the impact this has had on my own life and faith walk.

I thank and give honour to Pastor Jim Wilkinson and his late wife Cynthia, for their inspired leadership of Hollybush Christian Fellowship that has encouraged thousands to follow closely the Word of God in the Power of the Holy Spirit. I am deeply grateful for a life time of encouragement and friendship and the kind endorsement of the book.

I acknowlege with grateful thanks SeungeAe Ladd's amazing art work for the cover and the illustrations taken from the life of the Forge School that form the backdrop to the text. Also for her patience and diligence in helping with editing and moving towards completion.

Dedications

I dedicate this book
to my precious husband Geof
for his constant love,
support and encouragement
to finish
what God assigned.

This book
is also dedicated to all
who have journeyed to
The Forge School
and those who will
attend in the future,
to become as
a torch,
in the hands of
Almighty God
leaving
a living legacy
of God's Truth
to burn brightly
in the hearts
of future
generations.

CONTENTS

Introduction   **1**
Faith's starting point

Chapter 1.   **11**
Faith as a lamp connecting nations
and rekindling vision

Chapter 2.   **27**
Faith that fuels vision.

Chapter 3.   **33**
Faith that stirs out of the comfort zone.

Chapter 4.   **41**
Faith that brings focus

Chapter 5.   **51**
Faith's challenge-"Are you willing to be undone?"

Chapter 6.   **61**
Faith from meditation to revelation.

Chapter 7.   **69**
Faith that illuminates

Chapter 8.   **75**
Faith Alive

Chapter 9.   **83**
Faith is a place of reclamation

Chapter 10.   **89**
Faith for the nations

Chapter 11.   **97**
Faith in searching, suffering and silence

Chapter 12.   **109**
Faith forged on sure foundations

Chapter 13.   **121**
Faith's legacy and prophetic fulfilment

Chapter 14.   **127**
Faith is surrender and restoration

Introduction

"Faith's Starting Point"

"Here I am." The journey of Faith begins and ends here. This is a simple statement declaring the Name of the One who claims us for His own. The Great, "I am" the Creator of the Universe and the giver of life itself. At the same time these three words encapsulate the reality of absolute surrender. A willingness to listen and a heart that pounds to the beat of the Father's heart, knowing that without His breath the next step is not possible.

Abraham called the "Father of the Faithful" and "Friend of God" was branded by those names because he had been forged in the fire of God. God called him by name, "Abraham" and he responded, "Here I am"[1] The test of faith was to lay all on the altar. All his hopes and dreams which had been locked up in the child of promise he waited for so long and knew he had to be prepared to let go!

---

1) Genesis 11 v 1

Abraham and his son Isaac ascended Mt. Moriah together. Isaac carried the wood for the burnt offering and Abraham holding the fire in his hand and a knife. Isaac spoke to his father, and said, "My Father" and Abraham replied "Here I am son".[2] The Great "I am" will provide, His name being Jehovah-Jireh, the Lord our Provider.

Abraham builds the altar, binds his son and lays him on top of the wood. Before the sacrifice could be made by fire, it must be killed, and the knife was raised over the head of Isaac.

"The Angel of the Lord called out to him out of Heaven and said, "Abraham, Abraham" and Abraham replied, "Here I am."[3]

God hears the desperate cry of "here I am", and the pounding heart that says "I can be no other place, for where You are is the place of my obedience. I am living up to Your ask."

So, the blade poised to slay a precious son, was now kept for the "provided one". The ram, which at that moment was caught in the bushes. Nearby, and which would prefigure the lamb of God who was slain for all and whose cleansing blood would flow freely for the generations to come.

The legacy of faith lives on through all those who will

---

[2] Genesis 22 v 7

[3] Genesis 22 v11

dare to say "Here I am. I am willing to lay everything down to embrace the Hope of the Nations, Jesus the Precious Lamb of God." The real test of faith is to respond to the Call of God.

This book is written to give honour to the Great "I am" who calls His sons and daughters to the mountain of sacrifice, to the foot of the Cross. To discover at that place their true identity as sons and daughters of the living God who has a specific call and destiny for each one of us. Whether we are sixty-four or sixteen, God still hears us when we say from the heart, "Here I am." He forges us in the fire of His consuming love for us and shapes us for His purposes.

> *"He makes winds his messenger,*
> *flames of fire his servants."* [4]

Abraham and Isaac journeyed together and I invite you to make a journey with me to The Forge School of Faith in Llanelli Wales and discover for yourself how "A Living Legacy" can live on in you that was in the heart of Rees Howells, Intercessor, who was raised up for a critical time in the history of the United Kingdom and whose legacy lives on in a new generation of those who are willing to be forged for a life of true worship, intercession and mission to the nations. Forged by the master's hand and strengthened by His Spirit to overcome all obstacles

---

4) Psalm 104 v 4

in order to reach every creature with the Gospel in this generation. For all who walk by faith are the true seed of Abraham and are prepared to go lower that He may take us higher to live up to His ask, that we might be blessed to be a blessing.

"I will surely bless you and make your descendants as numerous as the stars in the sky and as the sand on the seashore. Your descendants will take possession of the cities of their enemies and through your offspring all nations on earth will be blessed because you have obeyed me."[5]

What a promise to Abraham and to all who walk by faith!

Abraham said, "Here I am" and yet someone of a much younger age had also heard his name spoken from the mouth of God.

He was a young boy called Samuel who is awakened in the middle of the night with someone calling his name. At that time, he did not recognise the voice, but he thought it might be someone he knew, so he runs towards the one whose voice he thinks it is, that of his spiritual mentor and father in the faith Eli, and responds to the call with the simple words "Here I am".[6]

When after the third time of hearing, he is told that it is God who called him and that if God calls again, he must

---

5) Genesis 22 v 17, 18
6) 1 Samuel 3 v 5, 6, 8

respond, "Speak Lord, for your servant is listening.[7] Samuel immediately obeys. But what he hears this time is a prophetic word concerning the household of Eli, the priest of God, who had failed to restrain his sons when they behaved badly and this would incur judgement for the neglect of responsibility and privilege, thereby dishonouring the Holy Name of the Great I am.

After God has spoken to Samuel, he lay until morning and then opened the doors of the house of the Lord as if to let the breeze of Heaven blow upon him because to carry a vision, or a prophetic word from God carries with it the responsibility of passing that word on just as it has been given.

His father in the faith calls him by name "Samuel" and again Samuel replies "Here I am"(v16). Was that simple response now said in a different tone? The first time, it was God who was speaking, and to say "Here I am" to Him would have carried with it the feelings of expectancy and wonder that God should want to speak to a young man. Was this time different? When we say "Here I am" knowing that it carries a weight of responsibility to say exactly what God has instructed with nothing hidden, are we as eager then to say "Here I am?"

I am writing this book for those who perhaps have heard the call of God, but not always recognised His voice. And those who have heard the call and who want to step

---

7) 1 Samuel 3 v 9

beyond their fears and answer the call to obey the voice of God no matter what because the Great "I am" has spoken and His plans and purpose cannot be ignored because they involve God's best for each one of us. Others may read this book and feel that at one time they responded to the call, but the cares of this life have crowded out their dreams. Or it may be that you feel one season of your life has ended and you are asking yourself, "Has God still got something He requires to do in me and through me, in a new season?"

Before the Bridegroom comes for His precious bride can we say, "I have known what it is to live in God's best in this life and therefore I am ready.

"Come Lord Jesus?" Or have I neglected my responsibility to reach the next generation and brought death, like Eli, when I could have brought life? There is no default position. There is no sitting on the fence. It's time to take the walk of faith. Time is running out for recalculating as the Sat Nav speak-over says when you chose to take a road that you think is better than the one your Creator had in mind before the world began.

"For He chose us in Him before the creation of the world to be holy and blameless in His sight." [8]

How many times has God had to recalculate to get us back on track with him? Let the legacy of faith live on in

---

8) Ephesians 1 v 4

you as you begin the journey, I invited you to say quietly before God, "Here I am".

I believe God will meet with you there and lead you to the place of being forged ever deeper into His heart. For in the fire of His presence our hearts are purified, and our lives are made as a polished shaft in His hand that is fired to reach its intended goal.

Be aware of your uniqueness as you begin this journey for everyone's journey to the Forge will be different. For some it comes in the flush of youth, when focus is clear and sharp, and the journey is yet another adventure of discovery. For others it will come in mid-life when tensions have torn at your heart strings and brokenness and pain have crouched at your door and you need to find a place where healing can take place and a flame of love rekindled. For others it will need to come at a time of transition when one season has come to an end and a new season is about to begin.

We all have to find our way there via the Cross? There are no short cuts.

For it is only at the Cross where mercy and grace flow freely and where the everlasting flame is ignited and new life begins It is there where one is struck by a love so amazing that you cannot walk away from it all you can do is recognise your need of it.

Jesus Christ, was struck and beaten to an inch of his life and then crucified. He chose to take the punishment we all deserved so that the coldness and hardness of our hearts could be softened and ignited with a love that can redeem us from our past and restore us to our future in Him.

"Who being in very nature God, did not consider equality with God something to be grasped, but made Himself nothing, taking the very nature of a servant being made in human likeness. And being found in appearance as a man, He humbled Himself and became obedient to death – even death on a cross! [9]

This act of self-less love was to reconcile us all to God so that we could live in the fullness of our true identity and purpose in Him. Yet the amazing fact is that before the foundation of the earth this plan of redemption was in the heart of God for the living flame which sin and satan had tried to quench had ever been and always will be available to teachable hearts that are willing to say "Here I am."

The poet Christopher Smart (1722-1771) wrote a poem entitled "Faith" and in the first verse he writes this challenge,

---

9) Philippians 2 v 6-8

"The father of the faithful said,

At God's first calling. "Here am I";

Let us by his example swayed,

like him submit, like him reply.[10]

---

10) "Faith", a poem written by Christopher Smart (1722-1771)

CHAPTER 1

Faith as a Lamp – connecting nations and rekindling vision

"For Zion's sake I will not keep silent, and for Jerusalem's sake I will not remain quiet, until her righteousness shines out like the dawn, her salvation like as a blazing torch." [11]

It was near October time when every devout Jew would go up to Jerusalem and Celebrate the Feast of Tabernacles. I am not a Jew but my friends, from an Israel Prayer Group were challenging me, "Don't you think you should go with us to Israel this time?" "I'm not sure, I replied, "but I will pray about it." But my mind was saying, "There isn't any money to pay for such a trip and yet I knew God had provided many times before when I was invited abroad on mission trips to Kenya and Romania and my husband I had little financial resources. Perhaps God will do it again in this new season of life called retirement?

"Is there such a thing as retirement in the Kingdom?" I pondered. "Has God still got something for me to do and I

[11] Isaiah 62 v 1

need just to obey His call, even though I don't know why Jerusalem?" Could it be that rather than retirement this might involve "Re-fire-ment". I hoped so as I longed for more of God and the excitement of travelling with Him to new places, I was not really ready for a rocky chair!

Early Sunday morning on 17th July 2011 I sought God about the matter. "What is your will Lord, you know me, better than I know myself, I always love travelling with you but I don't want to go if it is not your will. Things sounded to be heating up in the Middle East as news reports spoke of Israel being surrounded by enemies on every side. Would it be wise to go at this time? It's amazing how many reasons or excuses for not going can invade your mind when you are being challenged about responding to a call.

I had been two years previous to Jerusalem on a prayer assignment with friends and it was a place I loved and longed to go back to but was this the right time? Dare I believe that I would have the joy of going again? I sat and waited for God's answer.

I felt I heard a still small voice saying firmly,

"Go up to Jerusalem
and I will show you more of my heart."

"Go up to Jerusalem
and I will reveal more about the light and where to take it."

"Go up to Jerusalem
and I will give you more revelation of my love."

These all came in such quick succession and having a pen poised as I often do when I am waiting for God to answer I wrote them down in my prayer journal. I read them over and over again and thought to myself "that sounds pretty clear" three times in a row "go up".

But often doubting myself, I asked, "Lord would you confirm it in your Word?" The question sounded stupid as I had rarely heard God speak quite so clearly and decisively in the way He had just done but God knows our weaknesses. He knows when doubt and fear crouch near to our door. He is patient to bring us to a point of recognising without any shadow of a doubt that He has indeed spoken. I opened my Bible and there in front of me were these words-

"One who breaks open the way will go up before them; they will break through the gate and go out. Their king will pass through before them, the Lord at the Head." [12]

"… Come, let us go up to the mountain of the Lord, to the house of the God of Jacob, He will teach us His ways so that we will walk in His paths." [13]

I ran downstairs where my husband was having his own time with God and breaking in like an impetuous child I asked, "What do you make of this?" thrusting my journal excitedly in front of him. He read slowly and carefully what was written and then in his typical farmer

---

12) Micah 2 v 13
13) Micah 4 v 2

type, down to earth way said. "It looks like you have to go up to Jerusalem." How will it be possible?" I asked. As far as I knew we had no money for such a trip, as trips to the Holy land at Festival times are much more expensive than at other times and we were just adjusting to life living on an old age pension.

"Well" he said, "don't you remember Auntie promised me in her will, I would receive £3,000 for being her Executor and I had already allocated half of that to you when it comes, so that should pay for your trip." Overjoyed I hugged him and said, "Do you really mean it?" and knowing he did I hugged him again. I asked, "Don't you want to go too?" You would love it there?" but he replied, "I have not been told to go," So that was that. "You will have your friends to go with you so you will be in good company."

My heart welled up within me as I ran back up the stairs, "Lord, now I have a very clear answer and you have made a way where I thought there was no way. How often have you done that and yet even now I have doubts, forgive me Father for you are so faithful and I am so slow to learn." I felt God heard my heart and filled it with His great joy.

The time drew new for the journey to be made which would be from my home in North Yorkshire up the A19 towards Peterlee to meet with my young friend affectionately known as "Sunshine Sue." Sue, small like myself, but with a smile that spans the ocean and brightens every place she goes was to meet me and we were going to fly out together from Newcastle airport to Tel Aviv. I knew she was as excited as I was to be making this journey together. We would meet up with other friends in Jerusalem who were travelling from different airports.

Before I could go, God led a very special couple to me to tell me that they knew why I was going to Jerusalem. I was intrigued. Then it became clear, as they alluded to the previous year when I had been entrusted with a precious gift of a Menorah. This magnificent Menorah had been purchased for a humble-hearted housewife, called Susan Gathercole, from Thirsk, a woman with a passion to pray for her nation and for Israel. She had been overheard in a 24/7 prayer room in Jerusalem, crying out to God for England. Asking God to remember the good things the nation had done and forgive the bad things it had done in going back on the promises it had made to Israel during the wartime.

Two American ladies had overheard Susan's cry. One was Princess Fawn who was last in the tribe of Pocahontas and another lady called Mrs Richardson. They told Susan that they wanted to buy her something to take back to England. Susan naturally thought "Oh they must want to buy me a little Menorah or something as a souvenir to take back to England." Little did she realise that she would be taken into a store to be told she could choose any Menorah she wanted. She was advised on a particular one which stood about three feet tall beautifully fashioned in gold and silver. It took two of the party she had travelled with to carry it home in their suitcases back to England.

The day I heard the story of this gift from one nation to another was a cold Saturday morning in January 2010 when I risked life and limb along an icy road that ran alongside the race course in Thirsk to Hollybush Christian Fellowship, also known as Miracle Valley. To my amazement twenty five others had turned up on that snowy day and it was my first meeting there to pray for Israel and I had not a clue what to expect. So when I heard about the amazing gift from one nation to another of such a beautiful Menorah, I felt a real stirring inside as this seemed an amazing transaction.

I said, quite abruptly, "I feel this is very significant to have such a wonderful gift given from one nation to another." Significant because of all it represented of the Light of God to the nations. Immediately, Pastor Cynthia Wilkinson agreed and said, "We must receive this gift and all it represents and I would like you to plan an appropriate service, celebrating the Light of the World. So in June, of that year, I invited a Messianic Jewish Rabbi to come and dedicate this gift, thanking God for the Light it represented in Jesus the Light of the World the true Messiah and Saviour who gathers together the nations and who had forged this link in Israel to ensure the light and lamp of God goes round the world before His return. The Menorah would act as a constant reminder to people to pray for the Peace of Jerusalem.[14]

The generous couple who knew about the giving of the

---

14) Micah 2 v 13

Menorah to Susan Gathercole in Israel, told me that the original vision of passing on a Menorah from one nation to another was birthed in Israel by someone believing it was a prophetic sign of the light going round the world until Jesus the Light of the World returns, and they believed I had to go to Jerusalem to purchase a Menorah to give to another nation.

I was not prepared for what happened next, as a roll of money was pressed into my hand for such a purchase. My mind was racing, now I had an assignment, how exciting was that, but which nation? I would have to pray, "Out of all the nations of the world Lord, who should receive such a gift from the United Kingdom?" I spoke in the silence of my mind, knowing God heard, for my heart was at peace. However, I felt as a child who longs to open their Christmas gift to find out what is inside. Finding it hard to restrain the temptation to guess or ask for a clue.

As a double witness, to ensure the right nation received the Menorah I would ask the original recipient of the Menorah for the U.K. to pray with me to discern the nation that should receive a Menorah to take back to their nation. God never disappoints. It was not long before I felt God dropped into my spirit the name of the country as being South Africa. Remarkably Susan had been given the same country a few weeks earlier. The jigsaw was beginning to fit together. Now all I had to do was to keep alert to see which South African God would bring across my path whilst in Israel.

Several of our party were on a bus bound for Galilee on a glorious bright day and we were all feeling in high spirits. "Would this be the day I would meet the South African? My focus was clear and no matter what other excitement I had, the anticipation of being shown the one who should receive a Menorah as a love gift from England to South Africa was palpable. I had already met two South Africans at the hotel but had been given the same reminder Samuel the prophet was given when choosing a King,

"Don't look on the outward appearance..." [15]

The driver of the bus, before he set off, shouted out, "How many nations do we have represented on the bus." His passengers began to shout out the different nations and my ears pricked up when I heard a small voice say, "South Africa." My head did an about turn to see where the voice came from and I noticed a woman sitting by herself near the back of the bus. Immediately I left my seat to go and find out.

It turned out that this lady was a leader of a prophetic dance group which had just toured all the States of America and she had gone home to South Africa, after the trip thinking, "Perhaps this is my time to retire" and then God called her to Jerusalem. She had very little time to make arrangements and on a restricted budget she was sleeping rough on the open topped roof of a Youth Hostel in Jerusalem. Someone had suggested she go on this trip

---

15) 1 Samuel 16 v7

to Galilee and paid for the trip. Miracles like this happen all the time in Israel and so she found herself taking an unexpected journey. My heart seemed to do a somersault. Then I asked her to excuse me for just a moment as I needed to pop to ask my friends at the front of the bus something but I would be back promptly.

Going to the front of the bus I said to the two Sue's, "I think I have found the person from South Africa, please pray as I go back to her." As soon as I went back and sat down, I began to tell this stranger about what had happened the previous year when the gift of the Menorah to our nation had been given. Then the Holy Spirit fell and my new found friend suddenly started weeping uncontrollably and I could not continue the conversation either because I was so overwhelmed by the Holy Spirit's presence. Tears of joy rolled down our faces like unstoppable rivers. "When we get to Galilee," I said, when we had both managed to collect ourselves, "I believe there is a Menorah there that I have to purchase for you to take back to South Africa." She looked incredulously at me and began to weep again and exclaimed, "I cannot believe this is happening to me!"

Arriving at Galilee, a place I had never been to before, I found a shop and before my eyes, high on a top shelf, gleamed a Menorah which was a replica of one which had been purchased for England, just slightly smaller.

I explained to the Manager, I needed the best deal he could give me. The price he quoted was the exact amount I had been given. He also added extra gifts which meant I would bless the people back home. How amazingly kind is God! That day Susan Gathercole decided she would like to be baptized as a sign of repentance on behalf of the United Kingdom for the sin of forgetting to honour the promises made as a nation to the State of Israel. As she came out of the Jordan, her face glowed with the Glory of God that was visible to us all.

The South African lady, called Daphne, unfurled a beautiful silk banner the size of a blanket which she had brought with her, depicting the Lion of Judah, and we held it against the backdrop of the water and the people in white robes coming out of the water. The sun shone down as the banner unfurled with the iridescent light of promise on each one as they came up out of the water.

How I enjoyed this day seeing the fulfilling of an assignment completed which God had set. I then discovered that the Pastor from China who had anointed and prayed over the Menorah Susan had been given was also at the same conference we were attending, which meant we could ask him to anoint and pray over the Menorah, purchased in Galilee, destined for South Africa. Our new found friend Daphne, could now carry back the Lamp of God and all it represented to South Africa and seek God for herself as to whether she would need to come up to Jerusalem next year to purchase a Menorah to pass on to another nation. For what had begun in Jerusalem as a vision was now being carried across the world before Jesus the Light of the World, would return at the end of the age, just as the prophet Isaiah said,

*"Nations will come to your light,
and kings to the brightness of your dawn."* [16]

When God said, at the beginning of time,

*"Let there be light" and there was light.
And God saw that it was good."* [17]

When we act on God's Word, light is shed on our path and something new is birthed in us to dispel darkness and uncertainty and enable us to enter into a new season with renewed joy and hope.

The Divine appointments given through the exchange of gifts from one nation to another coincided with the birthing of a new chapter in my life. For the next day God caused me to encounter a man whose story would point me in the direction of a new faith journey where more of God's fire would come to stir in my heart. The man was South Korean with the memorable name of Kyoo Dae Lee (Qday for short). Susan Gathecole surprisingly said, she knew this man for she had met him on the Isle of Lewis when she and her husband worked there. So my ears were on high alert as to what this man might say for I knew the Isle of Lewis was a place where a mighty revival had broken out through the prayers of two women aged 84 and 82 way back in November 1949.

---

16) Isaiah 60 v 3
17) Genesis 1 v 3, 4a

Qday spoke humbly and yet powerfully of the mandate God had placed on his life which was to restore the spiritual heritage of Rees Howells, a famous Intercessor from Wales. Rees Howells had been used mightily by God during the Second World War to train up men and women of prayer that would go to the nations. He had established a mission focused Bible College in Wales and had acquired extensive property to help to bring Jewish children to a place of safety during the war years. He had hoped to bring 1,000 children from Europe but in the end only 12 came. Our minds guessed the fate of other children who didn't arrive. Gassed and burnt alive in unholy fires which were used to exterminate the 60 million Jews during the German invasion of Europe, during World War II.

During Qday's testimony my heart was pounding and tears began to flow freely. I wondered why this man's story should impact me so much. When his testimony concluded, I wanted to shake his hand. I thanked him for what he had said because I knew something was stirring in my spirit but I did not know the full impact of that meeting until much later. "Could I have your address to keep in touch?" was what I managed to ask after many others came crowding around him to shake his hand. Qday seemed somewhat overwhelmed by what was happening as this was something he had not planned or even expected. He was not a "big-named" speaker on a programme who had been flown in for the occasion. He was a humble man with a servant heart who was carrying a vision that was bigger than himself and which he knew

God would reveal as He submitted himself to the mandate he had been given.

One of the first things I did when returning home was to see if I could get hold of a copy of the book about Rees Howells Intercessor. I did not have to look far because my prayer partner had a copy which I could borrow so I set to reading it and could not put it down. I found I had to stop and take stock several times when reading the chapters. Tears would suddenly erupt and I had to reflect on why this should be the case. What was happening inside? I was not sure of the answers but I did know I was witnessing through this man's life a dimension of faith I longed to walk in.

Several months passed and I was prompted to dig out the details of Qday because I desperately wanted to know how the vision was progressing and I told him what had happened whilst reading Rees Howell's book which he had mentioned in Israel. He told me that he was about to start The Forge School of Faith in December 2012 and I could come along if I wanted. The thought excited me about being part of a Faith School but I wondered what my husband would think if I said, "I would like to go back to school"

Having not long retired from full time service as Methodist Minister in the Yorkshire Dales.

In fact we had barely been retired two years and had been busy over those years doing work on our home and adjusting to a new way of life. Alongside this restoration work came the blessing of being able to see more of our precious daughter Anna Louise and son in law Luke and witnessing the birth of our beautiful grand daughter Olivia Grace born 27th October 2010. Her birth heralded a new season in our lives and a new dimension of faith to walk in. No surprising that her name means "Anointed Gift of God." New beginnings marked by new birth is a phenomenon which I began to discover delights God. It was significant that the Forge Vision was birthed at the same time as the arrival of a second son to Qday and his remarkable wife Bridget.

The wind of the Spirit had blown into some dry and barren places of my life and birthed a blaze of desire to see God move again beyond the four walls of our retirement home. A place my husband and I found great pleasure in re-shaping after twenty years of absence, but the thought of being re-shaped and refined by God for a new season fuelled my sense of anticipation.

What would The Forge School of Faith look like and how could it open up new doors of discovery, concerning walking with God and in a new season of life?

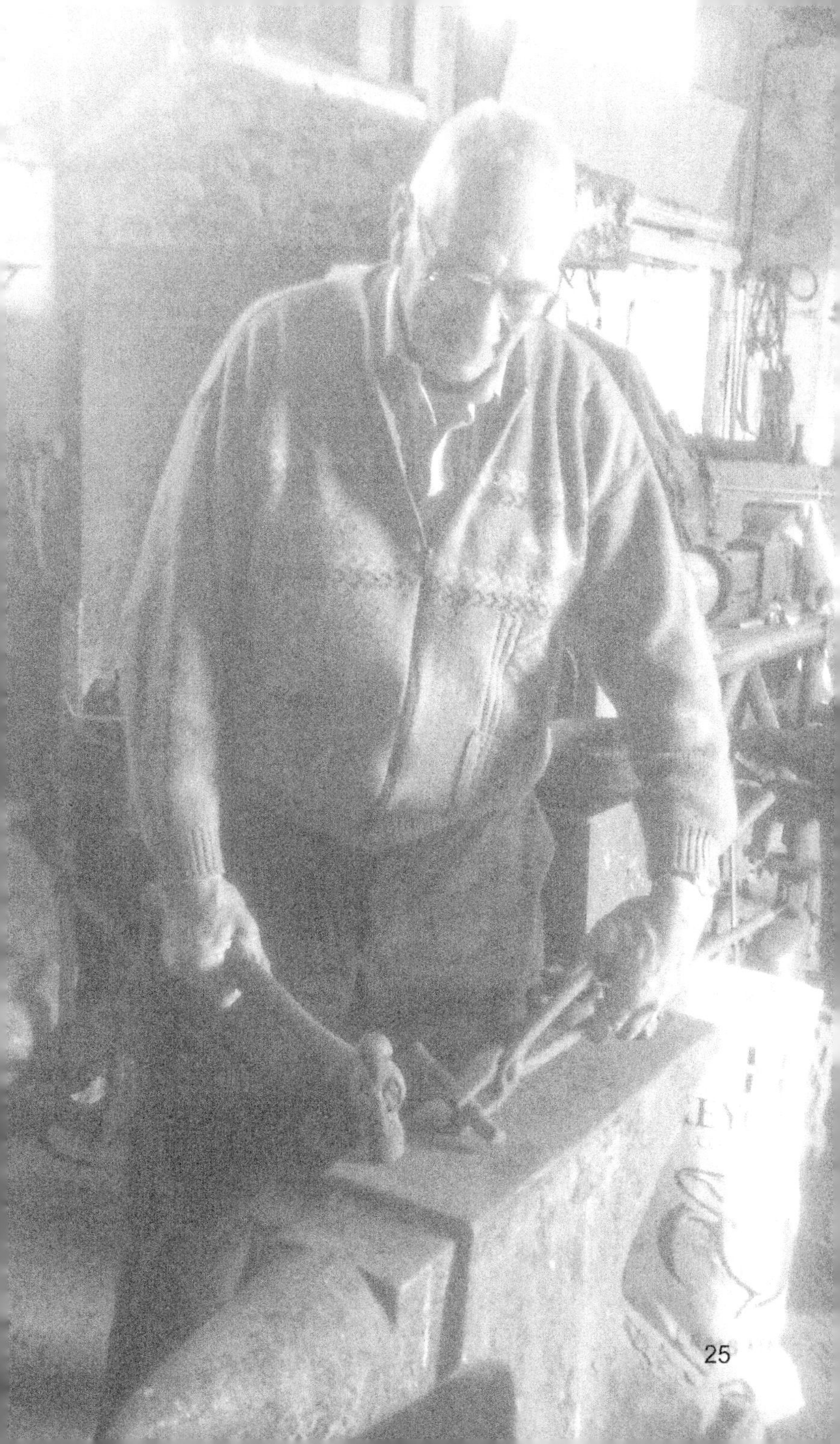

CHAPTER 2
FAITH THAT FUELS VISION

"Is not my word like as a fire?" says the Lord, "and like a hammer that breaks the rock in pieces." [18]

I was on the threshold of something new. A change from one season of my life to another was beginning to emerge and I found myself confronting the "Rocking Chair Mentality" that thinks "everything stops when you retire and it's time to do everything YOU want to do." "Well, you know God, I said, "I would serve you to the end but actually what I really meant was, till I was old enough to collect my pension!"

A consuming force was urging me not to settle for less than God's best or to fall in with the cultural norm. I knew I needed more faith to step out into this new season and the Forge School of Faith was the vision God had put in my path and the desire to be part of such a school intensified

---

18) Jeremiah ch. 23 v 29

as I prayed. The day came to mention to my precious long-suffering husband what I was feeling. By this time he was fully occupied restoring vintage tractors, which was a wonderful hobby, after his near fatal accident at work over 18 years previous. Whilst dipping sheep he slipped and fell into the six foot pit like trough full of Organophosphate Poison.

Franticly reaching for the upper edge of the trough, for he could not swim, he managed to haul himself out, on his third attempt. He had in his panic swallowed some of the liquid and yet had managed to get home, change his clothes and return to work. For such was his commitment and faithfulness to his God in the work he had been assigned. It was an accident but also a baptism of fire as the poison affected his immune system, rendering him unfit to return to farming being diagnosed with Organophosphate Poisoning, three years after the accident.

Still needing structure to his days he asked if I would let go of some of the housework and cooking so that he could have focus to his days. At the time I was serving full time as a Deaconess with responsibility for two rural churches. One of which was in need of demolition but the people there had a heart to rebuild. We also had a precious daughter of junior school age growing in her own faith and understanding of life.

The years had passed and we were all in a new season now. Our daughter being happily married and my husband and I returned full circle to a home we had left to respond to the Call of God. Geof was getting back the years the locusts had eaten as he was able to restore old "wrecks" of tractors he had accumulated over the years for such a time as "retirement." What happened in the natural with the restoration of the tractors was also happening in the spiritual realm as both Geof and I were being restored and healed to move forward in a new season. We had been through so much together of both joy and pain and I did not want to do something now if it would unsettle my precious husband's peace and healing. The mention of going to the Forge School and embarking on a new adventure was no surprise to Geof, when I mentioned it, as he probably knew, as only he could, I still felt I had much more to learn!

So come December 2012 I set off by train with my newly acquired Senior Railcard, which had entitled me to a third off the fare, heading for The Forge School of Faith in Llanelli, Wales. Journeying with me was my praying friend Susan Gathercole who had also felt that we needed to take the Menorah received in Israel to the birthing of a new vision. We were connected in friendship through this gift and the light of Christ it represented. Although the Menorah was locked in a suitcase to take with us, the light it represented journeyed with us. We found that everyone we met on station platforms and on trains started opening up to us and sharing their personal stories. We were able to see with the eye of faith how to speak into these situations and marvelled at how God worked in their lives as they listened to words of encouragement and hope that we had been given. We discovered afresh the truth of the words,

> *"Your Word is a lamp for my feet*
> *and a light on my path."* [19]

After travelling all day, we arrived safely on Friday evening in Llanelli station at around 4.50 pm. Qday greeted us with a winning smile and a respectful Korean bow gesture. Looking at our suitcases he must have wondered "Are these ladies stopping for a month and not just two weeks?" Sue and I realised after this journey we would each need to learn to travel light but this time around we were sure it was right to carry the Menorah with us. We trusted God would provide a Samson at each platform to lift our bags on and off the trains and we were not disappointed.

Although Qday could not be described as a Samson in statue we knew he was a giant in God for humility and grace shone through his welcome even though it took time to manoeuvre the cases into his small car. The next stage of our journey from the train station to his home in Llanelli was about to begin. We were in fact a day early for the Faith School but this did not matter for hospitality was readily available.

The smell of freshly baked bread met us at the door and we were welcomed in to a Shabbat meal lovingly prepared by Qday's English wife, Bridget. We were then

---

19) Psalm 119 v 105

introduced to Noah and Yohan their two young boys and other guests who would be taking part in the Forge School which officially started the following day.

An elderly neighbour, Welshman called Bryan, was also introduced to us. This was his favourite meal of the week and he looked forward to it greatly as much for the friendship it offered him as well as the meal itself. Love and laughter brought a common bond across all the different cultures. There was a great sense of ease in the conversation, as when cultures collide, and passion and purpose were embraced in the sharing of one another's faith journey. The breaking of bread and sharing of food saw the forging of focus in the richness of being part of the family of God.

If this was the "Starter" of what the Forge School offered then I could not wait for the next day when many more would be added to the table and the "Main Course" would be served.

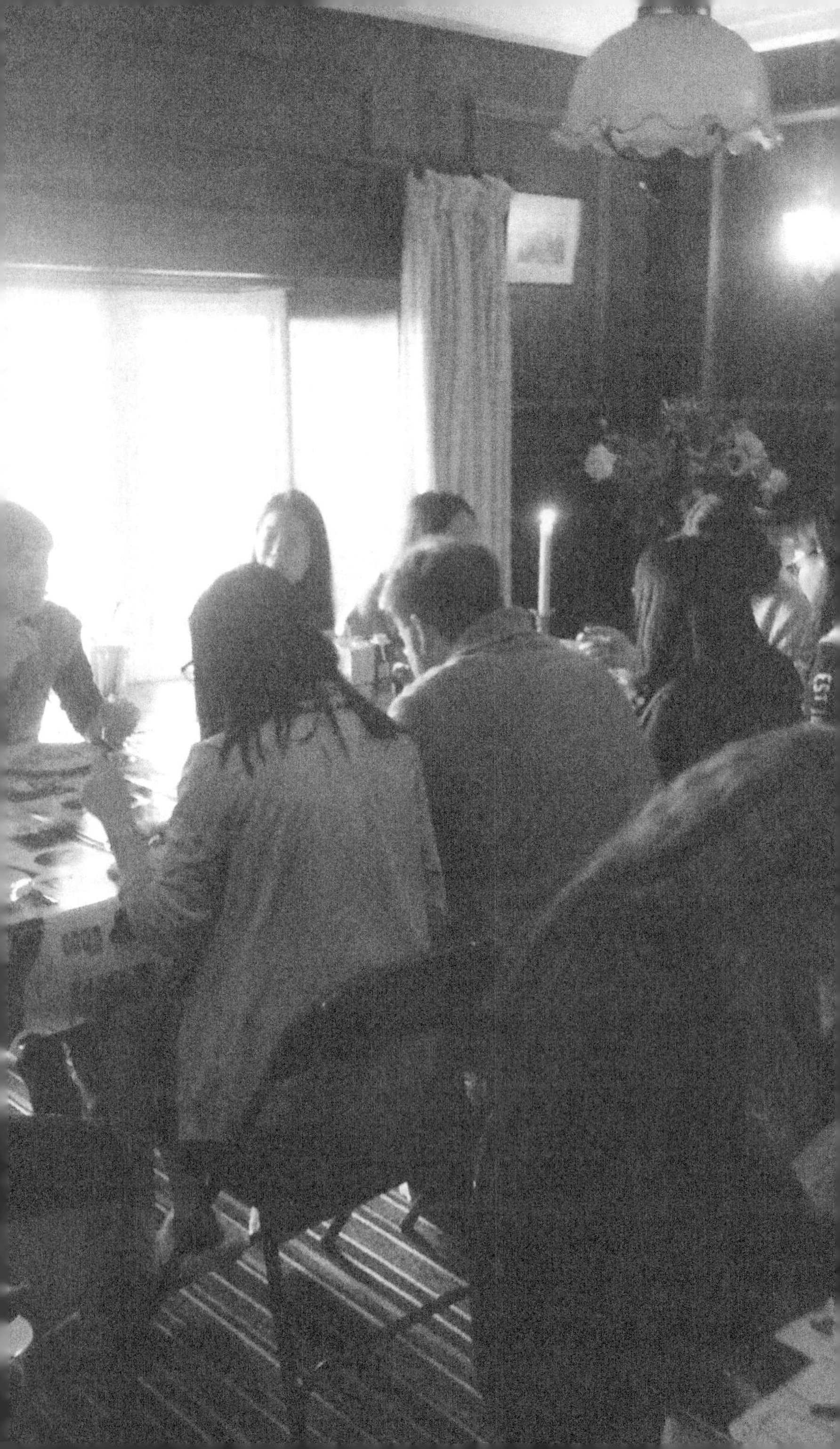

CHAPTER 3
Faith that stirs out of a Comfort Zone to the Forging Zone

After a restless night, due to the heady cocktail of excitement mixed with fear of the unknown, I awoke to find a household of activity moving boxes and suitcases near to the front door. "Where was everyone going and why all the baggage and boxes stacked near the entrance?" Slow cookers, boxes of cereals, fruit and vegetables waited to be transported. "Were we going camping?" I hoped not as my last experience of camping was a nightmare.

Then the answer came over breakfast, we were to travel to the venue where the Faith School would be held not so far away, in an old farmhouse. "Oh a magical mystery tour!" at least that's what it seemed like to me and Susan. "How many would be joining us?" What would it look like?" Many questions rolled around in my head but no time for answers. Today was moving day and everyone was ready to lend a hand to load cars, and set off for "The Forge School of Faith" whatever that may look like. We squeezed into the cars alongside the luggage and set off.

The heavily laden car made its way steadily along country roads until we reached a sharp turn left and it began to meander down an incline of bumpy road to a typical, painted white farmhouse nestled in the hillside. Welsh ponies and sheep graced in the fields around the house and on the craggy hillside. A spectacular rainbow overarched a tree in front of the house which seemed to invite us into a new day of promise as we began excitedly to unpack our bags and explore the house which was to become our home for the next fortnight. A sign had been laminated and placed on the rustic seat near the back door, "The Forge School of Faith" complete with the logo of a Blacksmith wielding his hammer to sharpen something on his anvil.

We each stepped through the old back door into a galleried passageway with wooden panelling half way up the wall on each side and various rural paintings adorning the walls. An old piano leaned comfortably against the wall down the passageway opposite a doorway leading to the dining room. Many of the boxes had to enter through the door to the immediate left of the back door which revealed a good sized country kitchen. Further along the hallway to the left was a large lounge with a big window that looked over the valley. The chairs that surrounded the room looked well lived in and faced a large black wood burner stacked at either side with roughly chopped logs. "How many families had sat around that fire on cold winter nights and what stories would they tell us of days gone by?"

Opposite to the living room to the right of the passageway was an oak panelled dining room complete with two large trestle tables adorned with brightly coloured linoleum tablecloths. It was a room that would soon resound with the clattering of plates, and the chatter of a gathered people who would share stories of their journey to the Forge School and begin to get to know one other over a home-cooked meal.

Often, when entering a place to stay, you want to find out where you will be sleeping and you unpack your bag and begin to breathe in the atmosphere of a new situation. So after taking a swift glance round the ground floor, I headed up the stairs which led off from the passageway. This was where Susan and I would part company because she had been allocated a different bedroom.

I was shown to a room which I would be sharing with three others. In the room was a double bed to the left of the door with a small gap and then a single bed in the corner. A large window with its own window seat looked out over the garden which stretched up the hillside revealing the rugged roadway we had just travelled down. An old fashioned wardrobe filled the corner opposite. A roof strut arched over a single bed which stretched lengthways against the wall opposite the double bed. In the corner opposite the door was a pot sink with an old fashioned washstand adjacent to it. The stand was not too dissimilar from the one my husband and I had inherited from his mum. In a strange way it made me feel at home so I chose the single bed near the sink, which had an old ottoman in front of a radiator with a four pin adaptor to plug in modern appliances, laid on the top.

The obvious omission to the room was a bath or shower but I was told that across the landing, I could find a shower room with toilet. My heart dropped at the thought of no bath as I just loved to soak especially after a long journey but this was an adventure so I was not too worried about being taken out of a comfort zone at this stage. I was quickly distracted from the thoughts of loss, and no bathroom, when two young women shrieked with girlish delight at the little treasures they discovered on their bed.

We all saw that someone had been in the bedroom before us and it was not the three bears of fairy tale fame, because on each neatly made bed were some goodies and a beautiful card individually inscribed with a prophetic word on each. The words were so apt on the card that it was like receiving an unexpected bouquet of flowers that bore a fragrance that reached deep into my soul and reassured me that I was in the right place. The bar of chocolate, tube of mints and a packet of paper tissues would be another form of comfort at a later moment but these little offerings of kindness spread a sweet aroma amongst us.

It seemed liked I was destined to be the granny of the bunch, among those bright young faces. The two girls I discovered would share the double bed in my bedroom. Both were from South Korea but one had a work visa in Wales, and the other was a teacher in Paris. I was told that another English lady would be joining us later and would occupy the other single bed.

Laughter filled the room as I tried to pronounce Korean names. I hoped the laughter would continue as remembering English names was sometimes a challenge and this new linguistic challenge threatened to haunt me for several days, but I felt like I could temporarily adopt them and give them an English name till I was brave enough to engage in the mental gymnastics of remembering different sounding names to anything in my memory bank.

Throughout the day the group expanded of mixed age range and gender which brought a sense of family and spanned continents, and made the old farmhouse buzz with life as its ancient walls were about to witness the miracle of the fire that forges lives as one in purpose and hope.

Leonard Ravenhill, a famous Evangelist once said: -

"You don't need to advertise a fire."

This Forge School of Faith, like others to follow, would draw people from many lands but the common factor uniting all would be the desire for more of the fire of God that brings passion and focus to life.

From America, to South Korea, a group of 20 people from many nations had been drawn to the One who has been described as "A Consuming Fire."

> *"Therefore, since we are receiving a Kingdom that cannot be shaken, let us be thankful, and so worship God acceptably with reverence and awe for our God is a Consuming Fire."* [20]

A beautiful log fire is great to sit near on a cold winter's night but who wants to be consumed by fire? This was The Forge School of Faith and every Blacksmith's Forge has a fire in which tools are placed to sharpen and shape for future use. Before I could think further on what this might mean, a shofar blast was heard calling everyone to our first shared meal as an internationally gathered community.

---

20) Hebrews 12 v. 28-29
Deuteronomy 4 v 24

*"Since we are receiving a Kingdom
that cannot be destroyed,
let us be thankful and please God
by worshipping Him with holy fear and awe.
For our God is a consuming fire."* [21]

---

21) Hebrews 12 vs 28,29 NLT

CHAPTER 4

Faith that Brings Focus

"It seems that every time the Spirit wants to move in a creative way He still has to find those who are "formless and void." Those with humility that comes from knowing they do not have the answers, which stimulate a holy desperation for God in them, for they seem to be the only ones who can ever be responsive to the Lord when He wants to do a new thing." [22]

The first evening meal together in the old farmhouse was full of laughter and the happy sound of voices getting to know each other. The new thing God was about to do in each of us would bring spice and cultural diversity, that would bring a fuller flavour to our lives and a capacity to risk more for God. We sang before the meal, giving thanks to God for the safe arrivals for food and fresh encounters which held the potential for faith to flourish in an atmosphere of expectation and joy.

It was announced at the end of the meal that we were to look out for the printed programme in the corridor

---
22) Rick Joyner - World Aflame p.15

which would give a timetable of what to expect over the fortnight. Also there was a schedule for you to identify which team you were in for household chores. Team A, B. or C. It did not matter whether you were in the Cleaning team, the Cooking Team or the Washing up Team as you would have the chance to do all three activities on different days. After all, we were to live as a family in community for a fortnight and housework does not do itself! We had not come to the Ritz Hotel to be waited on but we had come to The Forge to learn the true meaning of waiting on God which is both practical as well as spiritual.

Jesus himself said,

> *"Anyone who can be trusted in little matters can also be trusted in important masters."* [23]

Mother Teresa also said,

> *"Be faithful in little things, for in them our strength lies."*

Which she went on to explain means doing the best we can with the responsibilities and opportunities we are given.

When I looked at the programme for the fortnight I noticed a verse of Scripture at the top which intrigued me as I was not familiar with the first part of the verse but it sounded very fitting for a Forge School of Faith. It read:-

---

23) Luke 16 v 10
English Contemporary Version

"See it is I who created the blacksmith who fans the coals into flame and forges a weapon fit for its work. And it is I who have created the destroyer to wreak havoc; no weapon forged against you will prevail, and you will refute every tongue that accuses you. This is the heritage of the servants of the Lord, and this is their vindication from me, declares the Lord." [24]

Below this Text the programme was outlined with one Scripture verse for each day. I felt a deep sense of relief about this, although I was not sure why at the time. Perhaps it indicated a deep need in me to understand the meaning of rest rather than rushing through many verses without really getting to grips with what God was saying through one verse.

In the evening everyone introduced themselves and said a little bit about their journey to the Forge and then Qday shared the vision he had been given and explained further how he felt Isaiah 54 v16 was key to his understanding and purpose for the school. The picture God had given him was of a spiritual Forge, where apprentices learn how to handle fire, water, oil and metals and wrestle them into useful weapons and where the apprentices are themselves forged by the Word of God and the Holy Spirit's fire to become useful tools in God's hand. We were part of that vision by virtue of being there.

---

[24] Isaiah 54 v 16, 17

Qday prophetically declared that a huge tsunami was coming, so we needed to be prepared. This may mean, being prepared to be undone, reshaped, and moulded by God to be carriers of His Word, His heart to the nations. Both Qday and Bridget had had confirmed to them on three separate occasions that they would host a Forge School of Faith which would involve five main elements.

1. Sharing in Community Living

2. A lifestyle of Worship, Prayer and Intercession.

3. Bible Meditation and listening to God.

4. Faith Alive – practical outworking of Faith.

5. Exploring God's divine purpose for Israel and the nations.

These were all in line with the spiritual mandate, they had been given to redeem the land that Rees Howells once purchased and made the site of the Bible College of Wales, a place of intercession and training for the mission field, which was now vacant and for sale. The imperative came to Qday and Bridget to go and pray at the grounds of the College each week from January 2009. My mind pondered on the fact that every move of God in history seems to have begun by the seeding of faith filled prayers.

From January 2010 two more years of germinating and rooting of the received word and a dream which brought a sharpening of focus which had led to the laying of all on the altar, in relation to the physical legacy and picking up the spiritual legacy by way of starting The

Forge School of Faith. So we were all at the beginning of something conceived in the heart of God which involved picking up the spiritual legacy of Rees Howells to pray for our nation and the nations of the world and to submit ourselves to the forging process that makes transformation possible.

For me it is always exciting to be at the beginning of something new but in reality we are all pilgrims that are moving forward on ancient pathways that God prepared before the beginning of time that His Glory may be seen by each succeeding generation.

The evening of introduction to the vision followed our getting to know one another in an informal relaxed environment which set the scene for a fortnight of fun, forging and food! As well as the answer to the question for many of us, "Why am I crying?"

50

CHAPTER 5

Faith's challenge – "Are you willing to be undone?"

"Dear friends, do not be surprised at the painful trial you are suffering as though something strange were happening to you. But rejoice that you participate in the sufferings of Christ, so that you may be overjoyed when His glory is revealed. If you are insulted because of the name of Christ, you are blessed, for the Spirit of Glory and of God rest on you. So then, those who suffer according to God's will should commit themselves to their faithful Creator and continue to do good." [25]

Each day begins early in The Forge. The recommended time for going to bed was 9pm so an early start could be made around 6am and by 7.30am the old farmhouse fell silent as each person began to meditate on the one verse of scripture which was set for the day. My heart was pounding. Just one verse to look at but what was God going to reveal to each one of us from that one verse?

---

25) 1 Peter 4 vs 12-14, 19

> *"In the beginning*
> *God created the heavens and the earth."* [26]

Sitting in silence for a while and with pen and new notebook in hand it felt like I was being drawn into a conversation with God the like of which I have not had before or since because each encounter with God is uniquely relevant for that moment in time.

Little did I realise that this conversation would start to "undo" me as I allowed the fire of God's love to redefine my identity in preparation for a new season in my life.

This conversation, with the words of God in *italics*, I share with humility and sincerity to show the mercy and kindness of God to one who dares to ask questions and converse as a child to a Loving Father.

"It feels like I am a blank canvas Lord, on which you want to paint, I like the thought of that. Where do you want to begin?"

"In the beginning God! Nothing more, nothing less! I want to take you deeper in your understanding of Me, the uncluttered, yet the mysterious, the small and the vast. Think about what you need to do and let me draw you into a deeper understanding of who I am. Let me touch every part of who you are. Let me paint something new on the canvas of your life."

---

26) Genesis 1 v 1

"Where do you want to begin to forge something in my life?"

"I want you to learn to let go."

"What do you want me to let go of Father?"

"All the emotion and pain you have locked in over the years. Don't be afraid to let go. The tears won't obliterate the canvas, they make it ready for the colours I want to paint with, in this new season of your life." If I am to make you a part of a new foundation you cannot damn the flow, you must be made ready. I am Creator God and I am preparing the canvas where my river, my heart, can be expressed so don't be afraid when tears come and you do not know the reason why, when the painting is finished then you will see.

That sharp pain you feel in your head right now has to do with some of the things that have cluttered your mind and I want to begin there. As I take my paintbrush, I will be gentle as I erase the memories that have darkened your canvas. For it is springtime for you and I want to paint the colours of a new day that reflect this new season in your life and that has no shadows from the past. So let me begin.

"In the beginning God.."

"I know you like new beginnings as much as I do because everything is fresh and full of opportunity and potential. Just relax and let us see the picture that emerges as you submit your canvas to me. I am the master painter and every stroke counts."

"It feels like you're going to have plenty of water, for the tears of "letting go" keep coming. Some I know are tears of repentance. I'm sorry Lord for holding back the flow but I'm beginning to feel the release already. Can you use all these tears in the picture – what kind of foundation can be built on tears?"

"Remember I'm painting the picture and the water needs to flow, let it be available any time I need it!"

"I can breathe deeply at that, Lord, "In the beginning God.."

"You did not expect this beginning did you?"

"No, Lord! You are always the God of surprises and I have come to know that Your ways are better than my ways, your thoughts higher than my thoughts. So when the tears well up inside of me I will not stem the flow, I will trust that you need them to begin to mix the colours on this new canvas. Father what colour will you begin with?"

"Green."

"I gasped, "My forbidden colour Lord" You want to begin with green? I can feel the tears rising Lord as another memory surfaces. I was never permitted to wear this colour all through childhood, my dad would never allow it and yet Father, it's the first colour you bring to my canvas?"

"It's the colour of mercy, of growth and going forward. Yet you have known it as the colour of prejudice and hatred. The association of colour has been prejudice and blindness in

an era of Catholic and Protestant divide, the green and the orange. Sometimes you have not seen things clearly because of the prejudice born of lies, bitterness and contempt which has been the DNA from your family line.

Now I want to show you a different shade of green one that clothes the earth with grass. No blade of grass is the same, every blade is individual and unique. As I take my brush I clothe you with a new identity and every mantle of shame that was put on you, I remove so that there is no trace of forbidden colour which was not a true colour but a murky mixture that had coagulated in the bottom of a broken vessel and had leaked out onto you."

"In the beginning God created.., Father what are you creating here and now."

"A landscape that is green and expansive, that can embrace all nations, all people and Yes! You are in the picture. You are the tender green shoot rising. One that will nourish and nurture many. Not a blade of grass to be trampled on but part of my landscape for the end times. I have fed you in green pastures and it is time for you to lead others again to these pastures. Can you see yourself in the picture?"

"Lord, Im not sure yet where you have positioned me, will you draw me close so that I can see as you see."

"I am creating a landscape of limitless possibilities, where the forbidden does not obscure vision but the endless possibilities in this landscape will break off every restriction you have ever known."

"Creator God, is it important that I know what these restrictions are before I can fully engage with this new beginning?"

"Not at this time, just relax and enjoy the view, because when I make all things new there is no restrictions. Believe me when I say "No restrictions, no barriers you cannot cross, the whole landscape is for you to explore."

"Father, what are you creating me for in this new season of springtime."

"A vessel of honour for my Glory."

"Lord does that mean I am like that clay pot at the wedding feast full of water that you are changing into wine?"

"Yes, you are partly right."

"What is the other part Lord?"

"It is not what is or what was or even what will be, it is about that which has ever been. It is about my Glory, my Plan, my Purpose before all time began. It is about knowing Me with every breathe that you take and every step that you make which will lead you closer to my heart as you let me position you on the landscape of my love, my life, my laughter, my joy, my pain and my sorrow."

"Yes! This landscape includes many shades of green but what I create has the capacity to grow in the shadows as well as the light for in My shadow there is protection in the good

times and in the bad.

Have no fear the landscape has many colours but for you this day I want you to relax and enjoy the view as the colour of green the colour of mercy, growth, acceptance and knowledge of who you are and what I will show you in this moving forward time.

Foundations are being laid in you that can never be demolished because they are in me. This picture I am painting, which will continue to be a masterpiece of discovery as the bigger picture comes into view and you can see what I see a landscape of my creation."

"In the beginning God created the heavens…"

"The Heavens represent My goals and dreams, My love relationship with you and the whole of humanity. I have brought you to this place to see the stars that will light up the sky of this new landscape, the stars that will usher in my Kingdom purpose. The ones that arch the earth like my rainbow sign of promise. The ones whose eyes have also been dimmed and darkened, whose light has almost been extinguished by the gods of this world. I will show you through the tears where to find them.

It may seem a cloudy picture at first but I will send a strong east wind that will blow in the leaves of the trees which will bring a fragrance of spring time back to the earth. The Son will break forth with the glorious rays of new birth, flooding the earth with Glory, Majesty and Power. For I am the Lord of Heaven and Earth and when Heaven touches earth the landscape is transformed, I want you to be part of that picture, my child, are you ready to start again?"

"Yes Lord! Continue to let those rays from your Son illuminate and act like a laser that purges my heart melting and moulding it for this new season. I am so thankful that green is the colour of mercy. Tears that flow can fill a well which is made pure by God to help others to drink and be made whole. My heart echoes the feeling of the Psalmist who wrote:-

"O Lord,
You are the portion of my inheritance and my cup,
You maintain my lot.
The lines have fallen to me in pleasant places;
Yes, I have a good inheritance."[25]

The hour had gone so quickly and the meditation had ended but I wondered what others had received. After breakfast that journey of discovery began that added more to the picture. When we gathered in the lounge to share, without judgement, what we had each received as we had meditated, I was astounded by the richness of the sharing. How uniquely God had spoken to each and yet there was a thread of divine love flowing connecting us all. Vulnerability and honesty of sharing whether little or much allowed peole to be truly heard which brought a sense of community rarely felt in any other context.

---

25) Psalm 16 vs 5, 6 NKJV

Qday had raised the question, "Do you know why people do not want to start "In the beginning?" "It is because of the fear of failure people do not begin, but there is no failure in him!"

When you enter The Forge, the journey will be unique to you as God speaks in so many different ways and therefore you have no need to fear as there is no failure in Him. God does not repeat Himself. He prepared you to be the unique masterpiece of beauty and creativity through which His life can flow.

> *"For we are God's workmanship (Masterpiece), created in Christ Jesus, to do good works which God prepared in advance for us to do."* [26]

---

26) Ephesians 2 v 10

CHAPTER 6
Faith from Meditation to Revelation

"What did God do before the beginning?" He prepared –
"For He chose us before the creation of the world
to be holy and blameless in his sight." [27]

For those who attended the first Forge School of Faith we had no idea, what preparation we would need to make but the life of faith reveals a God who prepares and positions us so that at just the right moment He can reveal more of His heart to us.

Part of the process of meditation producing revelation is to listen in the silence, after reading a verse, until a question forms in your mind and then you allow the Holy Spirit to help you think and imagine what God is wanting to say to you through the text. Forging is not copying someone else, we are each being forged by the hand of God, to discern our own personal identity and purpose.

---

27) Ephesians 1 V 4

Blacksmiths discover that "Process doesn't take us to purpose, process is part of purpose." [28] It invokes rising early and allowing God to reignite the fire in your heart. It is about a willingness to be fuel in God's fire. As one wise former Blacksmith called Bob told me,

"Most tools made in a blacksmith's shop are made for somebody else. The pressure that comes in the process can range from half a ton to a kiss. Part of the Blacksmith's skill is to make tools which make other tools. Blacksmiths need a flexible mind to see things from all different angles, both inside and outside." He went on to say that he often found in the blacksmiths shop that the pieces of metal that had been discarded, thrown away, considered useless, were the very ones that were ideal for a job he had in mind.

How like God to take what the world considers as useless, and fashion them into something ideally suited for purpose.

"But God chose the foolish things of the world
to shame the wise;
God chose the weak things of the world
to shame the strong." [29]

Even Ehud[30], whose right hand was disabled, became a Blacksmith, making himself a sword. Christians cannot use ready-made swords, they have to discover the truth

---

28) A quote from a Sermon delivered by Dr. John Andrews at Hollybush Christian Fellowship Summer Camp.
29) 1 Corinthians 1 v 27
30) mentioned in Judges ch. 3

first hand from God rather than lean into other people's knowledge or experience of God. In a digital age it is easy to tap into information to fill the head with knowledge about something but Christianity is about relationship and revelation comes to the heart by the Holy Spirit. We need to choose God before Google. We need less information and more intimacy with God which brings Revelation.

In an information filled world it can be difficult to let go of the temptation to press a button and get other people's answers rather than seek God who is the answer. We may need to take a break from the futility of trying to build our lives on the sound bites of bricks of information rather than allowing God to make us a habitation of living stones.

> *"As you come to Him, the living stone*
> *– rejected by men but chosen by God and precious to Him,*
> *- you also, like living stones, are being built into a spiritual house to be a holy priesthood, offering spiritual sacrifices acceptable to God through Jesus Christ."* [31]

When a firm foundation of faith is established in you as you walk in relationship with the Living God, no matter what fires rage, you can still overcome. Four Jewish slaves who were taken captive to Babylon knew what it was to meditate on a God whose power was beyond measure who could help them triumph even in troubled times. The King at the time was Nebuchadnezzar, who made a gold

---

31) 1 Peter 2 v 4,5

image measuring ninety feet high and nine feet wide, perhaps to match his ego and desire to see all his citizens brought into ungodly alignment to his self-appointed god image. His edict simply stated was:-

"Whoever does not fall down and worship will immediately be thrown into a blazing furnace." [32]

The King's law had to be obeyed but three brave men, Shadrach, Meshach and Abednego did not compromise their faith in a time of crisis. When called to defend themselves for not obeying the edict they bravely replied to the King.

*"O Nebuchadnezzar,
we do not need to defend ourselves
before you in this matter.
If we are thrown into the blazing furnace,
the God we serve is able to save us from it,
and He will rescue us from your hand, O King.
But even if He does not, we want you to know,
O King, that we will not serve your gods
or worship the image of gold you have set up."* [33]

The courageous Hebrew slaves even though they had been educated and been made to imbibe the culture of a pagan nation, and their names had been altered to stamp out part of their identity and faith, they remained strong in their relationship with their God. Even when bound and thrown into the fiery furnace, they come out unscathed,

32) Daniel 3 v 6
33) Daniel 3 v16 - 18
34) Daniel 3 v 27

with not even a hair of their heads singed; neither were their robes scorched and there was not even the smell of fire on them. [34]

These three men depended on the revelation of what they knew of God by faith rather than the information which threatened destruction, and instead of being burnt by earthly fire, they were protected by the Holy fire of God's presence.

Even the King witnessed that he saw four men and not three in the furnace and the fourth,

"is like the Son of God." [35]

Likewise their compatriot Daniel, who his captors renamed him Belteshazzar, prayed unashamedly before his God during the reign of King Darius. Daniel so distinguished himself among the Administrators, for his exceptional qualities, that the king planned to set him over the whole kingdom. Unholy fires of indignation and jealousy were lit and other Royal Administrators collude to have the King make and enforce a decree that would bring Daniel down from his high office.

However, we see in Daniel a man who knows his God and who stands under the shadow of His protecting love as the mouths of the lions are kept shut when Daniel is thrown into their den. Unholy fire or ferocious lions are not a match for the God who reveals Himself to His own in

---

35) Daniel 3 v 25 KJV

astounding ways.

The forging God does through hard and testing circumstances in the people who seek to know and honour Him more brings maturity of faith as the believer learns to depend on the faithfulness of God and the truth of His Word.

God brings flexibility to those who are willing to allow the hammer of His Word to shatter old mind-sets and traditions that have imprisoned and rendered them useless. He re-fires and reshapes so that a personalised sword is made, effective in His hand. The process begins as we learn to rest, relax and be real in His presence. Learning to relax in the love of God and listen for His voice and heartbeat through meditating on His Word becomes a foundational gift that the Faith School offers to those who submit themselves to the process of forging.

Meditation that brings both Revelation and Creativity is both life giving and transformative to all who engage in this discipline.

Joseph, a man who had been wrongly imprisoned for rape, received a revelation born of his meditation and relationship with God. He knew God could interpret dreams. Through his awareness of God in a difficult situation he dared to believe that he would one day walk free. While meditating on Joseph's plight [36] the following poem was birthed:-

36) Genesis 39 v 12-40

When Revelation Comes

Mercy dawns by compassion's embrace

Heaviness lifts by God's grace,

Light dawns from nights of pain

Hope Soars by Heaven's gain.

When you are wondering what life means

Understand this, I know your dreams

For I give birth to your desires

From a flickering flame to a blazing fire,

WHEN REVELATION COMES

None can darken, dampen or destroy

The purity of My River of Joy

That pours incessantly into your cup

When you choose to lift it up

THEN REVELATION COMES

For I am the lifter of your head

To restore hope when it was dead

When offence had overtaken

And you felt yourself forsaken

THEN REVELATION COMES

Did Joseph catch a glimpse of Glory

As he told the Butler's story?

Just three more days of incarceration

And he would see the interpretation

AS REVELATION COMES!

Yes! It always comes to those who wait

Seeking beyond your sorry state

Looking beyond life's circumstances

Finding how your God romances

AS REVELATION COMES

CHAPTER 7

"Faith that illuminates"

"And God said, "Let there be light and there was light."[37]

Illumination brings revelation for when the Holy Spirit comes, like a laser light cutting through steel, it sharpens perspective and wisdom.

This phenomenon happens all the time in The Forge as people yield themselves to the process of transformation through engagement with God's Word. Shrinking back is not an option. To become an end-time Blacksmith, it involves staying close to the fire of God's presence every day.

"See it is I who created the blacksmith who fans the coals into flame and forges a weapon fit for its work..."[38]

It is recorded in John's Gospel that

"In Him (that is Jesus), was life, and that life was the light of men."[39]

---
37) Genesis 1 v 3
38) Isaiah 54 v 15
39) John 1 v 5

As people dare to be real with one another in an atmosphere of safety and non-judgemental acceptance there is a glorious illumination that comes in the honesty of sharing. No contribution is considered too small, in fact few words can often contain the profoundest of meanings i.e. every pen has a small tip or point , without which it is rendered useless. We all need each other and when we value the contribution of each, we are all sharpened.

> *"As iron sharpens iron,*
> *so one man sharpens another."* [40]

This sharpening is a dual process, through interaction with God and with one another we gain possession of that which God has promised. A Kingdom which is not of this world but which is built by God as we submit ourselves into his hand, we gain the fullness of the inheritance of identity and purpose laid up for those who love Him.

> *"It was not by their sword that they won the land,*
> *nor did their arm bring them victory;*
> *it was your right hand, your arm,*
> *and the light of your face, for you loved them."* [41]

There is a sense of God's favour and blessing that comes through interacting with the truth of God's Word and seeking to apply it to daily life.

Light brings definition and distinction to individuals and the roles and responsibilities God assigns to each.

---
40) Proverbs 27 v 17
41) Psalm 44 v 3

with that illumination hope, strength, encouragement, security and worth are gained. For some it is a case of rediscovering that which has been lost and darkened by seasons of selfish pursuits, pain, persecution, burn-out and loss. This is not about position or status as the world defines it; rather it is about embracing the fact, that it is all about Jesus, and the release of His life and light through each servant heart.

The Psalmist said,

"The entrance of your word gives light..." [42]

It is as we allow the light of God's word to penetrate our inner land that we discover who we really are. A child made in the image of God but whose image has often been marred, and veiled by the shadowlands. We often turn towards the shadows in an attempt to run away from the light. The times of evasion of responsibility, the times of rebellion and self-centred pursuits all take us away from the light.

Even though a seed begins life in darkness to come to maturity, it needs to reach for the light, as we all must do. Although God formed light He also created the darkness. [43] As the seed had to learn to live in silence and darkness for a while so must we break through the womb of the night to the dawn of a new day. Waiting for the moment of transformation and revelation that the light brings to

---

42) Psalm 119 v 130
43) Isaiah 45 v 7a

those who are open to receive what God alone can give.

The creativity, which is born of God, to see something birthed in the darkness can be the privilege of those who are prepared, like the grain of wheat, to fall into the ground and die that new life may emerge.

> *"I tell you the truth,*
> *unless a grain of wheat falls to the ground and dies,*
> *it remains only a single seed.*
> *But if it dies it produces many seeds."* [44]

This involves a dying to self in order that the Glory of the Selfless One may be seen in in us.

We need to embody the truths of the Psalmist,

> *"You, O Lord, keep my lamp burning;*
> *my God turns my darkness into light."* [45]

> *"Light is shed upon the righteous*
> *and joy on the upright in heart."* [46]

When Jesus spoke to the people He said,

> *"I am the Light of the World,*
> *whoever follows me will never walk in darkness,*
> *but will have the light of life."* [47]

---

44) John 12 v 24
45) Psalm 18 v 28
46) Psalm 97 v 11

47) John 8 v 12

Those who allow themselves to be forged by God are those who will see that empty words, like an empty life cannot suffice. Only those who follow the one whose Word holds the light of life will discover a fullness of joy and see fruitfulness in their lives.

CHAPTER 8
Faith Alive

*"Do not merely listen to the word,
and so deceive yourselves. Do what it says."* [45]

Finding a place to learn to rest in a frantic and busy world is crucial, for from real rest flows action that is life giving and enjoyable. Learning to live in a family that God has chosen to bring together is a unique and thrilling experience.

So, the lifestyle of the Forge includes finding God in the routine tasks of cooking, cleaning and washing up in teams, where laughter and learning bounce off one another. Sharing a picnic at the seaside and games in the park on the day of rest that God assigned from the beginning of time in the weekly Shabbat (which means to restore/cease) brings an added dimension to home and family life and completes the cycle of rest and refreshing to handle the mundane with joy as each simple act done for God becomes a delight rather than a duty.

45) James 1 v 22

Every day provides an opportunity to activate your faith. Simply because The Forge is a School of Faith we have specific days within the programme called "Faith Alive." During the first week of the school the Faith Alive day is activated within the context of the school itself. The second half of the fortnight, Faith Alive is directed towards people outside the local community.

Kathy Kelly, one of the Core Team at the Forge School, a former Graduate of Bethel Supernatural School of Ministry in California, gives Attendees of the Forge a glimpse into what it involves in partnering with the Holy Spirit. Her teaching on "Listening to God" for Words of Knowledge and Scripture as well as pictures He may give, all help students to engage with great expectation in the Faith Alive Days.

Faith Alive days can be likened to a Treasure Hunt where God gives you clues which you follow till you find the treasure He has prepared in a person He wants you to meet. There is nothing more exciting than a treasure hunt especially when the clues given by the Holy Spirit are specific and clear albeit at first seeming rather random.

Like the day two of us had spent time in prayer, asking God for Words of Knowledge or pictures that would lead us in the direction God wanted us to go. The two pictures I received were strange to say the least. The first was like a Bishop's hat coming down from the sky and the other picture I received could not have been more random – it was an empty chip tray.

My friend saw a man in a red jumper also wearing a blue pair of jeans which had a hole in the right knee, sitting outside what seemed like a cinema building. I was impressed by her picture as I thought it was quite specific and there could not be too many men that fitted that particular description.

I was new to this way of doing things but I had faith to go on the adventure to explore what this conferring of authority from above might mean, symbolised by the bishops hat. Would spotting an empty chip tray on my journey also serve to lead me to encounter someone who was treasured by God?

As Jesus often sent His followers out two by two, Kathy and I paired up for that day. We walked through a park to an impressive looking building and I felt drawn to go inside. A counter formed a large semi-circle in front of me which had glass screens with an assortment of people behind them. "No bishops there", I mused!

Then just as we were about to leave I witnessed a man turn away from one of the counters heading for the door. Was this my treasure for the day? I had an immediate urge to go up to the man and speak to him. It was at that point I felt God was wanting me to introduce myself to him and to say something that took me by surprise and probably him more so. "God wants me to tell you that this is not a day of disappointment this is a day of new beginnings for you, as God wants to show you how precious you are to Him. God wants to bring you out of the mess you feel you are in and give you the strength to help you overcome the storm you feel in at the moment." This six foot amazon of a man with tears in his eyes took me by the hand and shook it. "I'm Owen", he said, in a broad Welsh accent. "I want you to meet my friend David who is waiting for me just along the street." At this point Kathy left me to go to look for the man in the red sweater she had been shown in prayer.

Although I was in a strange place, talking to people I had never met before I felt a calmness and peace upon me. The two men started to share their life stories at the entrance of a shopping precinct. Big Owen had only recently become homeless and his friend Dylan was helping him out. Owen had gone into the building where we met to see if he could get some financial support to buy some food to restock for his friend, but his request had not been granted so he was told to go back the following week.

Drawn together by adversity they were trying to help each other through a tough patch. They both had experienced times when they felt they had messed up with God and gone off track but I said, "We all do that at times but God is a God of the second chance, and our meeting that day was perhaps to reassure them that God would help, they just needed to turn to Him and ask for it." I asked if they were they up for that? They both eagerly said, "Yes!"

As people passed doing their shopping, two grown men closed their eyes in the street whilst I said a simple prayer. "God we've all messed up at some time but we believe you can get us on track again come and live in us today." To my surprise the guys started repeating exactly what I had said, with a loud "Amen" at the end of it.

A bishop's hat I saw in a vision, symbolised the conferring of divine authority had happened as the Kingdom of Heaven had touched earth as these two men opened their heart to God. Owen and Dylan's facial expressions, at the end of that prayer, was a tonic to behold they were both full of joy. Big Owen said, "I feel different!" What a treasure God had prepared for me that day, to witness two men wanting to get on track with God, they just needed to know God was on their case and He did care about them and they were ready to turn and admit the mess they had got themselves into and ask God to help them out of it. I told my two friends where they could go for a free coffee and off they went.

Thinking to myself, "Now where did Kathy go.? "Oh I remember!" She mentioned someone near the cinema during our time of prayer that is probably where she headed off to." I asked someone where the cinema was and headed in that direction, keeping focused on the next treasure. I had already been presented with two for the price of one in my first encounter, but I was still wondering what the empty chip tray I had seen in the prayer time was about. So I kept my eyes peeled as I began to stroll in the direction of the cinema where I could reconnect with Kathy.

I did not have far to go as there she was walking towards me through the shopping precinct. I asked, eagerly,

"Did you find your treasure?" She said, "Yes, but he was not willing to acknowledge that he might be on God's radar but his friend certainly was". So all we have to be is obedient and believe the words God gives us to guide us in the right direction but the outcome is up to God because the Glory is all His. When faith and obedience come together something good will always happen.

As we talked, I exclaimed, "There is my empty chip tray!" It was laid on a table adjacent to where a man was sitting who was wearing a heavy neck brace. Kathy knew the man and asked him how he was that day. He said he felt terrible as he was in a lot of pain, he could not move his neck. So she asked, "Would you like us to pray for you?" As we did the man's neck moved and his relief was palpable. He thanked God and us for stopping as the pain had gone and he could leave the empty chip tray and his pain behind. Neither myself nor Kathy can heal but we both know Jesus can and this man had faith and humility to ask for prayer. God honoured him and his willingness to be open to the Holy Spirit and we all thanked God for His miracle working power.

Faith Alive is about partnering with the Holy Spirit, obeying His prompting to act in response to the need. Later, when the school gathered, the rest of the school members shared their amazing times of connection with people throughout the day. At the conclusion of our sharing our testimonies about the "Faith Alive" we worshipped together and thanked God for His faithfulness and guidance. Faith is never boring, it is an active response to the love of God.

"The Word of God is living and active.
Sharper than any double-edged sword,
it penetrates even to dividing soul
and spirit, joints and marrow;
it judges the thoughts and attitudes of the heart." [46]

The Holy Spirit delights to do things through those who are willing to throw themselves on the promise of God, knowing that His words are true and can be trusted to bring salvation, guidance, healing and deliverance. We have nothing to give in and of ourselves but only that which God delights to pour through us of His mercy and grace.

Fear rather than faith will always prevent us from positioning ourselves in a situation that demands that we depend on God alone. But when faith is alive and active the power of God is released and change happens. God always honours faith, but without faith we can never hope to please God or witness His power working through us. Electricity pylons connect and carry power to illumine cities how much more can the power of Almighty God transmit power to transform and illuminate whole nations?

---

46) Hebrews 4 v 12

CHAPTER 9

Faith is a place of Reclamation

"The Lord is my shepherd, I shall not want.
He makes me to lie down in green pastures;
He leads me beside the still waters.
He restores my soul..." [47]

Every time we venture with God, the promise that the Good Shepherd goes ahead of us to prepare the way is there for us to claim. One such day is the trip The Forge School students take to Penllergaer. A place of great natural beauty of lakes and trees and wooded pathways, steeped in history.

Part of that history linked to Rees Howells, dated back to September 1938 when he had a burden to see the persecuted Jews of Germany and Italy return to Israel. The Lord also laid on the heart of Rees Howells a burden for the Jewish orphaned children who were made homeless because of the start of World War II. In prayer he heard the

---

47) Psalm 23 v 1 - 3

word "Penllergaer", which he knew was one of the largest estates in Swansea area. He found out that it was 270 acres and included a mansion, seven houses, a farm and many out buildings. He had hoped to house 1,000 Jewish children but in the end only 12 made it into the country because the war broke out engulfing the United Kingdom. The second Great War meant his dream to save Jewish children was not fully realised.

Our assignment from the Forge was to begin to pick up in prayer part of that unfulfilled legacy of Rees Howells and ask God to show us as we walked through the valley, what or how we needed to pray to engage with the legacy.

We were all part of a different generation wondering and imagining what it would have been like for children travelling from war torn areas to travel to this haven in Wales. I found an ancient carriageway along which the children might have been driven and wondered what their fearful hearts might have felt as they looked between the trees and heard the unfamiliar sounds around them.

Were they brought at night when trees can look like monsters reaching out their arms. Or was their trip in the day time with the sun shining through their wide eyes in wonder at the glory all around? I hoped it was the latter.

The day we arrived was fair but it had obviously rained the day before as the ground beneath our feet was moist and very muddy. I had not come prepared for the terrain so gingerly I clambered down a rugged hillside, with the help of friends, and through the wood to find at the bottom a stone pathway.

Eventually we came to a glistening waterfall where several young boys were daringly jumping from the top of the waterfall into the deep pool below. All jumped except one small boy who stood nervously with his feet on the edge of the rock. When it was his turn, his friends shouted encouraging him to jump. The small boy waited and waited and waited contemplating the long drop. A shout came out of me that surprised me "You can do it!" and off he leapt. As he did so, the echo of my voice boomed back at me from across the valley, "You can do it."

Could God really speak through an echo at a waterfall? In a talk earlier in the week we had been told that if we walk the land of Wales long enough even the stones would tell their story and if we sat by the waterfall it could speak to us. In a place like Wales, which has been steeped in prayer curiously anything is possible because God will answer the prayers of the ancients as our prayer becomes part of theirs. Then as we seek to reclaim the promises spoken over the land and its heritage for future generations, anything becomes possible.

God had indeed spoken to me in the echo from the waterfall as I had been feeling I could not fulfil a particular task which I felt called to do(i.e. Write this book), and it felt like God was wanting me to pick up the echo with the confidence of the boy who made the leap of faith from the top of the waterfall. Filled with the confidence born of

Faith in a God who never fails and who equips us for all He asks us to do, I logged this in my memory.

I decided to walk further. Accompanied by a young friend, we traversed along the pathway which meandered beside the slow moving river until the road narrowed.

We ventured into what seemed like an eerie enclosure circled by trees. The place was hung in mist, but there was none elsewhere and so with a young friend we stepped within the circle to notice a mound of wood. The remains of a large dead bird was splattered across what seemed like a wooden altar, with its torn feathers strewn all over the ground beneath.

My mobile phone immediately slipped from my hand onto the mound. I was horrified as I realised this was a witchcraft altar of sacrifice and it was the last place I wanted my mobile to connect with. After I stooped down to rescue my phone I looked up to see Matthew, a Messianic Rabbi, and one of our Teachers at the Forge, coming towards us.

We all knew we had stepped into a dark place. But before leaving we reclaimed the land in prayer asking the Lord of creation to cleanse it and make it a place of enjoyment rather that destruction.

With each succeeding year new generations of The Forge have prayed on the land and in seven years a massive transformation has taken place with many resting places being provided and cultivated pathways to discover new vistas across the lakes.

Now it is described as

"A Place of Beauty for all the family to enjoy."

Many other volunteers have come and cleared undergrowth and planted new trees and shrubs returning it to its former glory. There is no longer evidence of witchcraft sacrifices being made but instead the valley had been transformed to become a place for new stories to be told. A place where dreams can be formed and nightmares taken away. A place of joy and laughter and where children's wild adventures begin.

Perhaps it has recaptured the dreams and adventurers those Jewish children experienced in Penllergaer so many years ago all because one man dared to step out in faith in hard times to provide a refuge for a generation who would otherwise have perished.

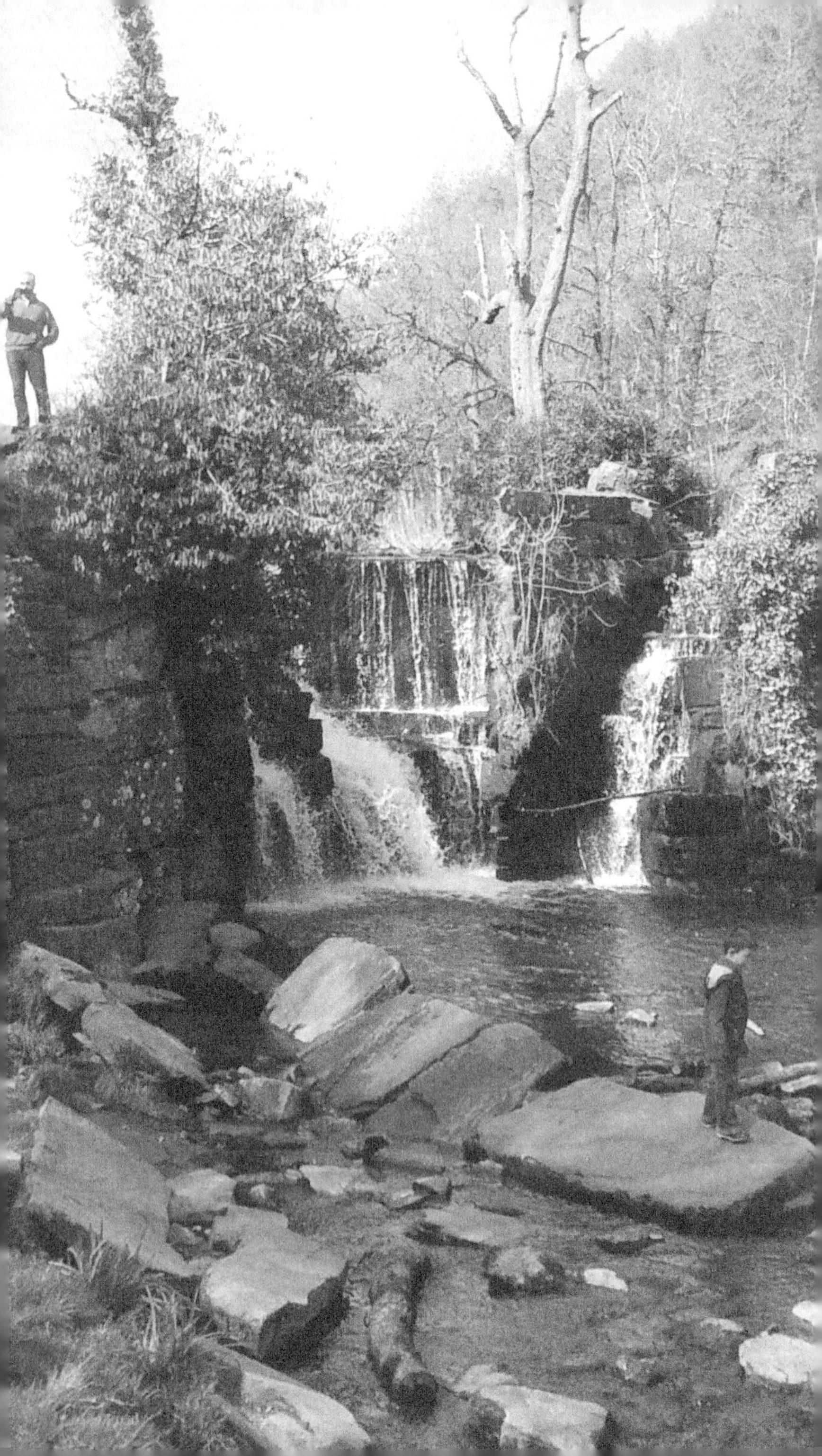

CHAPTER 10
FAITH FOR THE NATIONS

At the end of every Forge school there is the option for students to continue the forging process by being part of a three week Prayer Outreach into another nation. The nations highlighted by God through pray often have been nations which have or are currently experiencing great conflict and difficulty.

The first prayer trip for the Forge which was strongly on God's agenda was a journey to Iran and Iraq. This journey tested both the stamina and faith of all those who journeyed together but each person saw the favour of God through great connections which were forged with the people of those lands.

When you are sent as Ambassadors of Reconciliation, with hearts that are open to God, His compassion and love are released across cultural boundaries where breakthroughs and miracle connections happen. Provision of accommodation and hospitality came through people God had prepared to receive the blessing He had for them of encouragement and hope in hard times. Our declarations of faith and prayer become the seedbed of restoration for the refreshing of hearts and restoring the song back to hearts which have been hardened by the horrors of war.

Character is forged in the crucible of adversity. Often the personalities God is forming in the team are shaped through the particular set of circumstances that God allows the team to encounter. Journeying by faith is learning to trust God for the next place to lay your head, to trust for the food that will be provided, whether little or much and when you are used to a comfy bed and plenty of food in the fridge, the stretching of faith may come on the back of some mumblings and grumblings of the tummy as well as the mouth.

The Israelites did a lot of murmuring on their journey of faith through the wilderness. They had just exited Egypt and been miraculously delivered from the hand of their oppressors but the journey of faith through the desert, especially when water and food were not accessible, made the return to slavery a desirable option. From their journey we learn how easy it is to throw away freedom and inheritance because our flesh wants to enslave us with its demands.

"In the desert the whole community grumbled against Moses and Aaron. The Israelites said to them, "If only we had died by the Lord's hand in Egypt! There we sat round pots of meat and ate all the food we wanted, but you have brought us out into this desert to starve this entire assembly to death."[48]

---

48) Exodus 16 v 2, 3

Those appointed to lead a group, like Moses and Aaron may have to carry the blame for the mutterers and grumblers who don't want to speak up but instead choose to stir the pot of discontent if things don't go as they expected. However, faith grows when it is stretched and you learn to find faith's overcoming power when honesty and humility walk hand in hand through the difficulties.

Learning to keep short accounts with God and with one another is essential. In the midst of crisis situations in the world you can find God wants to break open new possibilities of change in long held attitudes and negative mind-sets when each team member is willing to submit themselves to God's reshaping process.

Times of team reflection and prayer at the end of each day lead into a new day of opportunities because prayer is the place where unity is restored. Unity in diversity brings incredible blessings of peace and strength to each member while the presence of God continues to guide the whole group out of the wilderness of negativity into a positive place where identity can be affirmed and a new way forward is opened up.

The particular Forge journey of faith I had the privilege of going on was to Israel. In Jerusalem, in the under-croft of an ancient church, a place had been set aside for prayer. The Leader of our group began to pray with individuals in the group each one receiving a blessing. The prayer over me was quite striking and unusual, "Let Vivien become as sand." was the phrase that stuck in my mind.

I had never had such a prayer said over me and I pondered on those words all day, wondering what they might mean.

At the end of the day, before retiring to bed, fatigue had set in and a cloud of insecurity seemed to settle over me. "Was I the weakest link on the team, was I holding the team back as I could not walk as fast as others in the heat? What did it mean to be as sand? Was I not what I should be in the eyes of the leader that he would want me to become something else?" Knowing the integrity of our leader I knew he was seeing a bigger picture so at the end of an exhilarating but tiring day I decided to hand my insecurities over to God and went to sleep.

During the night, I was woken up and felt God was showing me something totally new that was going to turn my thinking around. What I had perceived as a "put down" and negative statement, God was incredibly opening up a new reality as He showed me something of the significance of sand. I wrote down in my journal what I was given in the darkness of night which was to begin a change of mind-set that would alter me forever.

The Significance of Sand

Sand is significant because like stars, it is without number.

Sand is significant because it can contain water. It can hold it and it can also release it back to the sea.

Sand is significant because as the sun shines on it, it can provide a soft bed for those who would want to catch the sun's rays, those who need to learn to relax.

Sand is flexible, it moulds into whatever shape of foot that stands upon it.

Sand is significant because it can be used, when mixed with water and cement, to build the finest buildings.

Sand is significant because it has the capacity to carry the weight of a tractor or a tiny sparrow.

Sand undergoes thousands of poundings, washed by the waves, it becomes refined, purified, by the water it retains and gives away. It is prepared to be blown by the wind and positioned in the most unlikely places, it can even become part of the wall of a King's palace.

Could it be that "sand" is a metaphor for the person who is willing to be broken and reshaped over, the years by the washing over of the Word and the Holy Spirit as a life is submitted to God?

".. from dust we were made and to dust we shall return.." [49]

That night I felt God had touched an insecure place in me and changed a negative into a positive and caused a prayer to rise in me:-

---

49) Genesis 3 v 19

Let me be as Sand

Lord let me be as sand for You to walk upon

Let me be moulded by the imprint of your Son

Let me be as sand that clings to your feet

Responding to your voice, that makes me complete.

Let the Spirit-wind take me to where you are

To my next door neighbour, or to lands afar.

Where You are is where I want to be

As sand in time, through to Eternity.

Washed over daily by Your ocean of Love

Knowing always there is life in Your blood,

Crimson as sacrifice, consumed by fire

Like a candle burning to raise Your Name higher,

For when the wick burns and I am no more

Your light remains on Heaven's bright shore

I will know as a grain of sand, life's all about you

Each grain is designed for your Love to shine through.

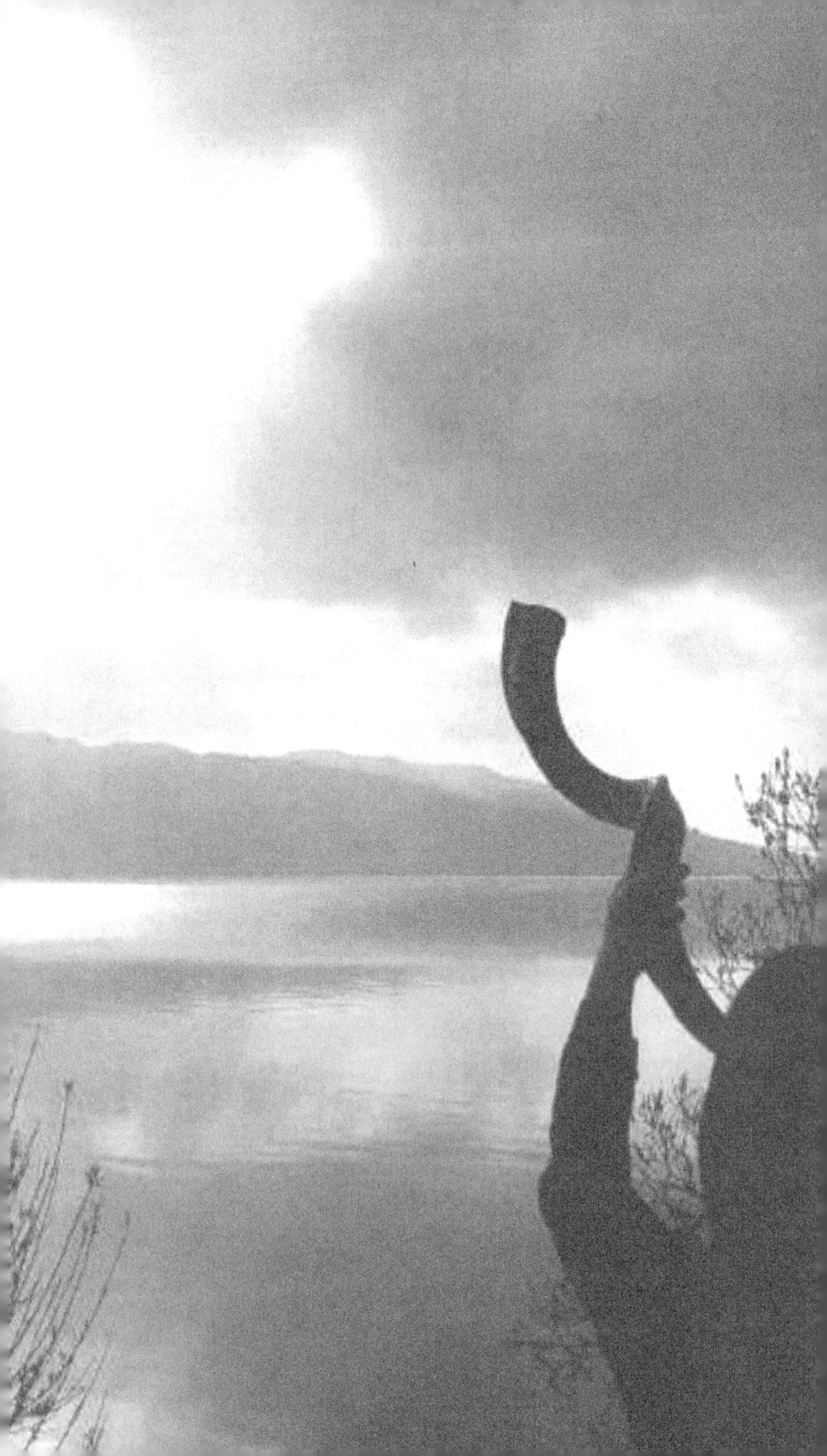

CHAPTER 11

Faith in Searching, Suffering and Silence

From the silence of a church under-croft in the heart of Jerusalem, where mention of sand had struck a deep chord of negativity, God mercifully shored up by changing the negative mindset into positive encouragement which made a new day possible.

Although the new day began in uplifting prayer and worship the weather outside had become wet and windy. During our worship we had a time of sharing and listening to God. The Holy Spirit made clear that our journey today would include a time of searching and silence which would speak volumes into our souls.

We felt first to visit an art gallery, which had its own precious moments of searching from the Lord and then entered "Yad Vashem", Israel's Holocaust Museum where silence was imposed on each visitor.

As a team of intrepid travellers we journeyed to the art gallery adjacent to the museum. It was an unusually windy and wet morning for Israel and so we embraced the warmth of the modern gallery and enjoyed the varied displays of paintings that lined the walls.

Paintings can help us to see the world as others see it. We all see things from a different perspective depending on what stage we are at in life emotionally, spiritually and psychologically. Different pictures can lure us to their landscape and captivate us by their vibrancy of colour and simplicity. We each chose a picture that had a particular pull for us to search its meaning or simply to gaze on its textures and colours and see what God might be saying to us through them.

After a while, I was intrigued to find a young man from our group standing transfixed looking at a plain yellow canvas which looked almost vandalised as it had three large dark slashes cutting through it. I waited until my friend was finished staring into it and I asked him what he saw in the painting. He hesitatingly said, "I am not sure, but I feel drawn into the spaces within the slashes."

That picture remained with me as did the comments of my young friend. During the night I had another wake-up call and felt led to write a poem simply called:-

The Picture with 3 Stripes

I met a young man transfixed in a striking way

Standing, pondering, for he could not turn away

"What is it that I'm seeing in such a sight so rare,

That I just need to linger longer,
 to simply stop and stare?"

God speaks in such a simple way to those
who want to listen,

A plain yellow canvas suddenly begins to glisten,

Three stripes or cuts in canvas
open up the spaces

Just like the wounds of Jesus
who humanity embraces.

God uses many ways of speaking
to draw us close to Him

The nail scarred hands, wounded side,
and cruel stripes that bring us healing.

"Was this Andrew's day of breakthrough?

Had God answered his heart-cry?"

"My son, I listened to you the day I chose to die!"

I saw your great potential
before you were in your mother's womb,

This day I raise you out of death to see life
beyond the tomb.

Yellow speaks of Glory
and resurrection all around

Now your heart can listen
for Heaven's Glorious sound,

For my voice is not only heard in language,

it's in the air you breathe

It's in the wind that gently whispers
through the trees

It is I who drew you to me,
one wet and windy day

So you could trace through a painted image,
what words I would convey."

The next day I handed the poem to my young friend. Neither of us knew the poem might have a prophetic edge to it. However, as we moved to Capernaum that borders the northern shore of Galilee, this young man encountered the One who bore the stripes on His back for love of us all. [50] Just as Andrew, one of the first disciples of Jesus, heard and responded to the call of Jesus to follow Him over 2,000 years ago, so Andrew from a new generation heard and responded to that same call to surrender his life, his future, into the hands of Jesus as Saviour and Lord.

Before our journey to Israel began, words of Roland Evans (one of the Speakers at The Forge) said, "We are all characters who live in God's poem." The truth of this fact was being evidenced in the synergy God was working in the hearts of the team to witness His miracle of grace as we journeyed together. Cultural boundaries were crossed and disparity of age made no difference as God unites hearts in the seeking after Him. In the searching and the silence faith grows as each one is willing to move forward learning from one another and submitting to the love of God that never fails and never ends.

---

50) Isaiah 53 v 5

Silence was compulsory as we moved from the

brightness of the art gallery to the shadowlands of "Yad Vashem" the Holocaust Museum. While we were there different emotions were tapped into as the team ventured through the corridors of time to encounter the horrors of man's inhumanity to man during World War II.

"No conversation allowed" notices, evoked an eerie silence expressed in empty eyes deep sunk in the faces glaring out of photographs of those whose destiny hand been snatched away by cruel hands and hardened hearts of their captors. Pictures of a different nature to the art gallery now bombarded the senses, exploding the emotions like shrapnel from a gun. Tearing at the heart strings and tormenting the mind that such crass cruelty could have for so long been ignored but was not catalogued in tunnel like corridors of misery.

A Journey through Time

I stood within the vortex of the entrance
to "Yad Vashem"
My eyes transfixed on a lady,
waving to me from way back when?

A brown cattle truck seemed packed
with flaying arms outstretched
But one ladies face and piercing eyes,
had me totally bewitched.

Was I being invited on a journey
with a long lost friend?
Or could I detect disaster dangerously
waiting around the bend?

My feet seemed set in concrete,
as the truck was about to leave
And yet I saw the waving hand,
and the eyes that seemed to plead.

My heart was wrenched with longing
and tears began to flow
Was it some mother's darling daughter or a friend
I used to know?

I could feel the train now moving
as if I was on the track
Body swaying from side to side
Not able to go back!

Suddenly I was shaken back
to reality's gaping door
With the realisation my friends
were not with me as before

The horror of that journey
that six million Jews had made
And I was just at the beginning
of miseries cavalcade

In silence I move slowly
into the corridors of time
Sensing and seeing suffering
of the most horrendous kind

Children's shoes discarded,
piled high in a hideous heap
The tortured, tangled bodies,
of so many, made my spirit weap

Mangled spectacles formed another
Monstrous mountain rare
And skeletal figures with sunken eyes
staring in stark despair

Endless, horrors of betrayal
from hearts that knew no shame
Tireless, tormentors,
Treating women as fair game.

One and a half million children
meeting an untimely death
Gassed, choked and smothered
till they had no breath

Bright yellow Stars of David,
lie contorted on muddied ground
Once a mark of identification
Now a blackened mound

By now my tormented heart
is longing for fresh air to breathe
To step beyond the confines
Of cruel callousness bequeathed

As if someone had heard my inner cry
beyond the evil machinations
I arrive at a concrete circle
Marking the Righteous of the nations.

The circle became a well for me
where I could let go of the tears
Which had been locked up, it seemed
For year, and years and years.

Light dawned at the end of a tunnel
I could feel a cool breeze blow
But this could not erase the memory
of those slaughtered long ago!

Such was the impact on the full Forge team, that each found it hard to speak to one another after the visit to the museum ended, as emotions were raw and real and each person needed space to move back into the present, beyond the pain, needing to find in the silence life's equilibrium.

New life always starts from darkness. As the prophet Jeremiah knew.

> ***"Before I formed you in the womb I knew you,***
> ***before you were born I set you apart;***
> ***I appointed you as a prophet to the nations."*** [51]

Without form and empty and yet God knew us, our true identity. God always knows us at the deepest level. The Spirit of God hovers over us to recreate our identity as it was at the beginning when He first knew us. No matter how empty or void the world was or our world may seem to be, this does not forego the fact there is still potential in us. Perhaps we need to ask.

"Am I empty enough for the spirit of God to hover around me and move through me, or am I too full of what I want to do, that the Holy Spirit has no room to move?"

" Do the sounds of earth deafen me to the sounds of Heaven?"

"Or can I in the silence of the womb of each day hear the heartbeat of God that prepares, forms and fashions?"

---

51) Jeremiah 1 v 5

God's fires don't need any ashes, His breath, His words, spoken through us can ignite and transform another person's world because God is constantly recreating and restoring from the fire and passion of His heart. God dwells in thick darkness even though He is light.

"... even the darkness will not be dark to you, the night will shine like the day, for darkness is as light to you." [52]

Does this not mean that if we are afraid to move out in the darkness of the unfamiliar and unknown God will be there with us as much as in the times we feel confident because the path is clear before us?

The activation of faith is always God's initiative as faith itself is a gift from Him. When we realise that, through our darkest hour God has walked beside us, this awareness should fill us with anticipation and expectation that what God has done for us He can also do for others and our part is just to share what we know of the nature of God.

Sadly we can sometimes expect God to come into our world with a blinding light or a crack of thunder but God loves to come quietly. He peers onto the scene of human suffering with the caring heart of a father and the gentle grace of lamb. We see the humility and grace of his entrance in a manger bed, born of the Holy Spirit, coming as the Light of the World and Saviour of us all.

---

52) Psalm 139v12

CHAPTER 12
Faith forged by sure Foundations

The Forge is seldom a silent place, nor is it a cave of Adullam [53] where you go to hide from your problems or withdraw from responsibilities. The Forge is a place of Community where individuals go to share their personal journey, relationship and spiritual understanding of God with other people who are prepared to do the same.

Moving forward in your Christian walk is guaranteed as your life is built on the sure foundation of knowing Jesus as your Saviour and Lord and choosing to keep an open ear and teachable spirit whilst the biblical building blocks are laid by those who come to teach and speak at the Forge on subjects foundational to living full and fruitful Christian lives.

The over-riding desire of each person who has served the Forge as Teachers and Speakers has been to be in tune with the Holy Spirit so that Glory is given to God. The

---
53) 1 Samuel 22 v 1, 2

ability to impart wisdom is worked out through discipleship and servant hearted leadership. For when the Holy Spirit is released the heart of Biblical truth comes into view and we accept God's discipline, guidance, commands, and His purpose and vision for our lives. For the Holy Spirit makes real to every individual what it means "to lay all on the altar."

Conviction and authority come from those who have learnt to obey the promptings of the Holy Spirit, putting to death selfish ambition for the sake of honouring the Word of God and taking its message to the nations.

> *"And they overcame him by the blood of the Lamb*
> *and by the word of their testimony;*
> *and they loved not their lives unto death."* [54]

So the teaching given is not purely academic but it has been lived out by those who teach it. Because of this, the teachings carry the authority, authenticity and anointing of the Holy Spirit which cultivates a passion for God, to work with Him rather than for Him. Craftsmen, like blacksmiths, in a biblical sense, means that everyone will engage in their God given task with the integrity, creativity and excellence which is born of God and gives Glory to Him alone.

"Vulnerability" and "Accountability" are part of the servant leader's gift to the group, which helps to lay a

---

54) Revelations 12 v 11

foundation so that others learn to share their story and to see where God has been present in it. The rhythm of the Forge School environment gives each the ability to move counter-culturally from the restless world and stop to learn what it means to move from the place of rest to work, rather than from work to rest. In that rest, is a trust in God that is willing to wait for His timing and purpose rather than give into the demands and pressures of the frenetic world in which we live.

Built into creation, was a time of rest which God patterned for us,

> *"By the seventh day God had finished the work*
> *he had been doing so on the seventh day*
> *he rested from all His work.*
> *Then God blessed the seventh day and made it holy*
> *because on it he rested from all the work*
> *of creating that he had done."* [55]

Every Saturday becomes a Shabbat Rest in the Forge, a time of relaxation and family celebration with a picnic in the park or a stroll along the sea shore. This special time of rest and renewal begins with a Shabbat meal at 6 pm on Friday evening. A deliberate stopping and switching off, of mobile phones or computer activity is made by many to ensure the day is kept special. The emphasis of building relationship with each other in a relaxed environment is paramount. As the Epistle to the Hebrews reminds us:-

---

55) Genesis 2 v 2, 3

> *"There remains then,*
> *a Sabbath rest for the people of God,*
> *for anyone who enters God's rest also rests from their works,*
> *just as God did from His."* [56]

Even the prophet Isaiah declared,

> *"…. In repentance and rest is your salvation,*
> *in quietness and trust is your strength…"* [57]

Jesus said,

> *"Come to me all you*
> *who are weary and heavy laden and I will give you rest.*
> *Take my yoke upon you and learn from me,*
> *for I am gentle and humble in heart*
> *and you will find rest for your souls."* [58]

To Moses, God said,

> *"My presence will go with you,*
> *and I will give you rest."* [59]

Resting in God is foundational to fruitfulness as the humility of Moses revealed, we cannot go forward without God because we end up in self effort and labouring in vain. Just as our inner land is renewed by rest, so the earth, (the outer land,) has been given permission to rest, according to the law given to Moses.

---

56) Hebrews 4 v 9, 10
57) Isaiah 30 v 15
58) Matthew 11 v 28, 29
59) Exodus 33 v 14

> *"But in the seventh year*
> *the land is to have a Sabbath of rest, a Sabbath to the Lord.*
> *Do not sow your fields or prune your vineyards."* [60]

This rest for the land was demonstrated to me on a mission trip to Israel when taken to "The Valley of Tears" where the Yom Kippur War had been fought over six days in 1973, once a barren land was now, a bowl of fruitfulness with apple orchards stretching as far as the eye could see. It was the sabbatical year for the land resting during its seventh year and therefore anyone could eat the fruit because it would not be harvested by the farmer who was obeying the Levitical law even in the 21st century.

Favour and fruitfulness rests with those who rest in God and who are able to turn a valley of tears into a valley of joy for strangers who could eat the fruit that would not be harvested that year. From a place of rest we can arise to give a natural response of worship to the Lord of the Harvest.

---

60) Leviticus 25 v 4

Worshipping and Waiting on God

Waiting on God in the morning,
Feeling His tender touch
No restless striving to erase
The embrace I love so much.

Sitting at the feet of Jesus,
Reaching to hold His hand
Beyond the veil I come to you
To find my heart expand

To know that you draw near to me
Each time I turn to you
My heart is set a dancing as
You make all things new

I want to know your inner depths
My Saviour and my Lord
More than I knew you yesterday
Your priceless love outpoured

So I listen in the stillness
Content to have You near
No other place I'd rather be
Your presence makes vision clear

The scales are lifted from eyes
On things I did not know
For in the light of Your Glory
New life begins to flow

I understand more deeply now
As Your company I keep
My eyes are opened to the truths
That make my life complete

Echoes of praise can be heard in the Forge House as the School participants arise to thank God through the singing of scripture before meal.

"The steadfast love of the Lord never ceases
His mercies never come to an end.
They are new every morning. New every morning
Great is Thy faithfulness O Lord,
Great is Thy faithfulness." [61]

Everyone holds hands around the meal table as the Grace is sung and the blessing on a new day is given. Worship unites and draws us near to God and each other and empowers us to move outwards to reach others near and far.

True worship is a lifestyle – it cultivates an attitude of gratitude that flows from and to the generous heart of God. Having my roots in the Methodist Church which was born in song by the influence of Charles and John Wesley, I found in the land of song, known as Wales, there was a depth of worship produced by the cross-pollination of cultures and a purity of worship brought in by the Korean participants of the Forge which I believe was born of sacrifice.

"Therefore, I urge you, brothers in view of God's mercy,
to offer your bodies as a living sacrifice,
holy and pleasing to God
this is your spiritual act of worship." [62]

---

61) Lamentations 3 v 22-24
62) Romans 12 v 1

Key people who have learnt the meaning of sacrifice are those who have sown into the Forge Vision. These are the "living stones" that have laid firm foundations for the Forge School of Faith.

Qday and his wife Bridget, being the founders of The Faith School, by their continued sacrifice and surrender show many how they can find their song of deliverance, healing and salvation by daring to forge ahead beyond manmade structures to focus on the Kingdom of God by adopting faith, worship and intercession as a lifestyle making room for all. The home schooling of their two boys Noah and Yohan in their early years have ensured that a new generation will arise knowing how to walk and live by faith as they have grown up with an ever expanding family of nations around them and loving parents who have nurtured them.

In the kneading and giving of fresh bread daily both physically and spiritually, in lifestyle, word and song, people can get a true taste of what belonging and acceptance really looks like as a foundation for living.

There is a creative expression of a new generation willing to carry the mantle of this trifold lifestyle of worship, intercession, and mission in the leadership of a young Welshman called Owen and a South Korean called SeungAe who was a former missionary to China and Thailand. This dynamic couple were the first to be married from the Forge House having met each other through the School of Faith. Their sacrificial love shows a new generation how to live joyously, creatively and with a passion for God that is both practical and worshipful as they seek to serve God together in the School and through building teams that can serve the community and go to the nations in years to come.

Rowland Evans, who pioneered the Missionary Training and sending organisation called World Horizons and Nations (training non-western students to begin their own indigenous missionary movements) came to the Forge School as an accomplished author [63] and teacher, passed on a lifetime of wisdom, experience and insights of his journey of faith in China and Tibet and others part of the world.

Speaking with authority and great humility of one who had surrendered himself into the hands of God and who by faith continues to this day to act on the call of God by sharing his faith journey with the broken and vulnerable people of Swansea who find themselves homeless.

Gail Dixon as an accomplished author [64] and teacher, the current Director of Nations has encouraged many to see breakthroughs by unstopping the wells of mission, prayer and fellowship in an event which has become a movement known as "Celebration for the Nations." Her biblically based talks bring great insight and wisdom to the Forge School participants.

A Messianic Rabbi from American called Mathew Toller, who now Pastors at an International Mission Church

---
63) Books "45 Minutes in China" and "My Sea is wide."
64) Books "Beloved warrior" and "Hidden Glory"

in South Korea has been a teacher, encourager, mentor, an accomplished author [65] and supporter of the Forge vision since its inception and has helped firm up the foundations and principles that have established the school. His teachings on Grace and Forgiveness have been key to unlocking a fresh understanding of God's heart and have brought release and revelation to all who have attended the School which has aided in their formation and forging into God's purpose and identity for their lives. His teaching on "How to live determined" is born out in his own life through his integrity and sacrifice in travelling thousands of miles by faith to help mentor and nurture all the attendees of the School. This all helps in the continuing pursuit and passing on the Legacy of the late Rees Howells intercessor.

A wonderfully perceptive and caring woman called Kathy Kelly stands between the door of the Forge School of Faith and the community as she has an ear to what goes on in the communities around the Forge household and has an eye to practical needs of the Forge by bringing in replacement furnishings etc. Through her training Kathy also encourages students to discover new strategies of engagement with people which includes waiting and listening to God for prophetic insights and then following the clues God gives to make that connection possible. Her teaching lays a foundation of heightened expectation for what God will do when people are prepared to risk all on the leading of the Holy Spirit. The faith building skill of

---

65) Books "Adventures in Cymru" and "Grace undone"

connecting with others stands the students in good stead when going to foreign nations. To be sent to the nations requires a total dependence on God at all times.

The undergirding of all the foundational principles of the Forge is done by various intercessors outside the School. These are those who have aligned themselves to see the forging process continue to future generations by daily committing the Forge Team to God in prayer.

Their work is unseen but not unnoticed by God, the effects of which help to make each School a unique experience to each person who attends. Two of these intercessors are Roland and Gail Roderick who have also taught at the school on the centrality of Israel to God's purposes and the need to understand its prophetic significance in relation to biblical prophecy still being fulfilled today.

The Forge School of faith recognises that everyone is in process and not yet perfect from the Founders and Teachers to the newest arrivals. However, the unity that is born of prayer, brings a blessing near to all who are willing to engage with the process of being forged by God so He can use each person as a tool in His hand surrendered and fit for Kingdom purposes.

CHAPTER 13

Faith's Legacy and Prophetic Fulfilment

"Now faith is the substance of things hoped for the evidence of things not seen." [66]

A fortnight in the Forge includes a visit to the Bible College of Wales.[67] The first time visited it looked derelict and forlorn, with broken windows and shrubbery growing out of cracks in broken cement work.

I asked myself, "What was the legacy to be picked up in this place of Faith, Hope and Love or had these three long left the building?" I was not expecting to see this kind of dereliction, after such faith filled beginnings in the time of Rees Howells. But here we were to sow again our prayers of faith for a new season, but only God knew what

---

66) Hebrews 11 v 1
67) The Bible College of Wales is once again being used to train and equip a new generation to impact the nations. Its walls mended, gardens tended and lands restored carrying on the vision God had given to Rees Howells all those years ago, as proof that He who begins a good work will be faithful to complete it. God always answers the prayers of all who are prepared to lay all on the altar and those who have a heart to build

he had planned and always with God in the place of death there are seeds of Resurrection.

I saw a heap of old suitcases stacked high on the grass ready to be burnt or carried away.

"What memories did those cases contain of people who had journeyed to the school from many lands long ago to reach this Bible College?"

Walking round the perimeter I saw a cross formed in wrought iron gates and also etched in wood panels. Surely this was hallowed ground and would remain so! Then my friend Susan Gathercole had a vision of two large lions guarding the gate to the main entrance.

That vision stirred faith in me and I dared to believe that we were here to align our prays with the Lion of Judah for the protection of the site that it might be used again for His Kingdom purposes and not sold off for some property developer's gain. If this was truly Holy Ground then God would watch over it until it was placed into the right hands.

The baton of faith birthed here needed to be passed on to future generations. At that point I stumbled over a wooden handle in the grass. I picked it up and pondered about what the passing on of the baton would mean through our praying that day. We continued to pray and sing right round the building and land, then we visited the big house across the road, containing the Blue Room.

This was the place where 24/7 prayer was made with such great effect for the United Kingdom before and during the war with Germany. It was now damp, with flaking plaster, its former grandeur was vaguely visible and yet the presence of God still tangible. We prayed and listened to Qday as he had explained it was here he had to lay all on the altar of the vision he had prayed into since 1999 for the total restoration of the whole of Rees Howells heritage.

A card was on the fire mantel shelf in the Blue Room with the words "Place all on the altar" a challenge to all who desire to see faith's legacy passed on.

It is a humbling thing to lay down something you have prayed into for many years but it is only in the dying that new life can appear. We were all privileged to be standing in that holy place, because of Qday and his wife Bridget's obedience to pick up something of the spiritual heritage by his starting The Forge School of Faith, not knowing then what it would look like, or who would be drawn to the fire.

I was very moved and quietly prayed, "Lord give me the courage to lay all on the altar once again and be prepared by you to pass on the legacy of faith to a future generation."

We left the Blue Room to photograph the huge stone monument outside, visible through the window, which had the words engraved on it:-

"Faith is Substance"

I felt grateful and humbled to be one of those whose faith was to burn brighter by virtue of a young couple's willingness to lay all on the altar and seek God again for their lives.

We wondered reflectively around the garden, noticing the ravages of neglect and trying to imagine its former glory. A place where once a little stream had flowed was now stagnant and clogged with undergrowth. A large greenhouse was overgrown by vines and strewn with broken plant pots. At one time it would have been, a hive of activity with seedlings being potted and plants being nurtured to beautify the expansive gardens.

We prayed for the unblocking of streams both physically and spiritually and for reclamation of that which now stood neglected and overgrown. We also prayed that the gardens and orchards would be brought back to life with an array of colourful, fragrant flowers and abundance of fruit.

It was not until I was taken to Ffald-y-Brenin, one free afternoon from The Forge, did I realise what the outcome of our prayers, offered in the Prayer Room formerly occupied by Rees Howells, would be.

For at this Christian Retreat Centre and House of Prayer in the Presili Hills of South Wales, the first person I encountered was a lady from Singapore. It turned out that she was an intercessor whom God had quickened in prayer to visit Wales to spy out the land that would soon be purchased by her home church, Cornerstone Community

Church in Singapore.

It was no coincidence we met in the place of The Grace Outpouring where many miracles of connection are made; not least by those who visit the Cross that was planted overlooking the valley there. We stood and prayed together in the garden, thanking God for the divine appointment of shared prayers for the restored legacy of Rees Howells at the place of grace outpoured in the landing of singing, intercession and missional revival.

FAITH IS SUBSTANCE

CHAPTER 14
Faith is Surrender and Restoration

*"For God so loved the world
that He gave His only Son
that whosoever believes on Him
shall not perish but have everlasting life."* [68]

My time at The Forge was nearly over, but an unforgettable visit was made to "The Cross". Surprisingly this was a cosy farmhouse where hospitality was warm and inviting. Located on a piece of land lovingly farmed by Bob, a wise shepherd, and his devoted wife Bernice who loves to lay a table of home baked Welsh cakes and have the kettle boiling on an Aga stove to welcome visitors as they arrive.

This couple were friends of Matthew, the Messianic Rabbi, and teacher at the Forge and he was so excited to introduce the Forge Family to this couple who shared a wonderful gift of hospitality. On a cold winters day we

---
68) Lamentations 3 v 22 - 24

wrapped up well for the visit but we soon had to shed our coats as we huddled into their warm and cosy kitchen.

I was soon to learn that "The Cross" was so much more than a farmstead; for this couple had been through their own forging experience with God which was now bearing fruit, leaving a legacy for future generations to enjoy.

Bob had been a farmer most of his life but he also had worked in the mines and as a blacksmith and when the coal board closed the mines Bob was forced to retire and give himself one hundred percent to developing the farm as tenant farmer for one of the landed gentry. It was like a jungle when he took it over thirty three years previous but with diligence and hard work he cleared the land one hundred and fifty acres in total, as the farm increased.

Shepherding six hundred sheep Bob rarely needed a sheep dog for the sheep would come whenever he called them and they would follow him. The disobedient ones were pulled to one side and placed in a position where they knew their need of a shepherd and after three days they followed him and those once rebellious sheep became the leaders of the flock.

The sheep were not the only ones pulled to one side, for a moment came in Bob's life when he knew God was drawing him closer to His heart to experience the power of the Cross of Christ. Bob had a dream where he saw himself making a strong wooden cross. He knew that when Jesus said,

*"If any man will come after me,
let him deny himself,
and take up his cross and follow me."* [69]

He also meant you must carry the cross in your heart and your mind. It was about total surrender; doing things God's way, every day.

The morning after the dream Bob got up and everything he needed to make a cross was waiting to be used in the barn. It took a couple of days to make. He was going to carry it to the island that he had made twenty years previous with massive stones retrieved whilst clearing the land, which now stood surrounded by a pond which was naturally formed. However, the island was now covered with brambles and weeds. The stones which were the foundation of the island were now invisible. After coming back from checking the sheep Bob heard clearly three times,

"Bring the stones back to life!"

It took three days to transform the island and clear all the rubbish away. But Bob knew the voice of the Good Shepherd and he had to obey instructions, not knowing what the final outcome would be. He placed a plank of wood as a bridge across to the island so there would be access to the Cross when he had positioned it.

---

69) Matthew 16 v 24

From the farmhouse to the Cross was a winding track that started off from a wide open space and narrowed as you got closer to the island, which reminded me of the story of John Bunyan called "Pilgrims Progress." The day Bob set off with the Cross to the island he took with him a shovel to dig a hole to stand it in. It was not long before he could feel the cross biting into his shoulder and he was about to put it down but did not want it to touch the soil.

He sharply reminded himself of his Saviour and all He had done for him in going to the cross and he wept and continued the emotional walk to the island.

On reaching the island Bob chose to close his eyes as he knew he needed the guidance of God to position the cross. With eyes tightly shut, he turned round several times and set off whispering "Now God, please guide me." Before he knew it he could feel the plank of wood under his feet and was over on to the island and he turned round a few more times and felt a prompting to stop and open his eyes and where his right foot landed he was to start digging.

He was surprised to find as he opened his eyes his right foot was positioned in a central point on the island and as he started digging three foot down it was soft like peat and after gathering some small stones he positioned the cross where God had assigned.

On leaving the island another miracle was evidenced. Bob, noticed the reflection of the cross on the water and no matter which direction he walked the reflection followed him. He could not have worked that out in a thousand years mathematically but God knows whether we as a people move to the right or the left and His love is persistent in pursuing us that we would know the glory of surrender and transformation that comes through the miracle of salvation as we come to the foot of the cross.

It was not long after this that a death of ambition had to take place in Bob's life as the farm had been allocated for the establishment of a solar farm. This meant another shift and dying for Bob for the once green pastureland would be covered in glass panels to catch the light from the sun and be changed into the energy for people's homes in the future.

The way of the Cross is never easy but it is always worth it. The Way to the Cross Bob had created and developed was allowed to remain running through the farm. All the wooden pallets which the solar panels had been transported in, were resourcefully refashioned to insulate the barn and make display units which housed the retelling of the Bible stories in new and innovative ways for families who would come to visit the farm. Some were made into simple crosses and placed into the hands of children and visitors that they may ask themselves where they were in relation to the cross?

The adjacent field to the barn, was ploughed out and shared to be come a Fellowship field for the people from many nations. Each group who came was given a strip of the field to grow vegetables.

We as a group from The Forge were privileged to be there the first year after the cross had been positioned and a whole Pilgrim Way had been made. From the wide gate near the farmhouse, to the narrow gate across the bridge to the island, where the Cross took central place would be a journey many generations would make.

On that simple journey many signs had been positioned along the pathway, giving scriptures which became stopping points of contemplation.

I made that first journey to the Cross with Joosun a beautiful South Korean lady, young enough to be my daughter, who had seen a Forge in a vision before she ended up as a student of The Forge School of Faith. We stopped at each sign and took turns in reading the Scriptures. It was a cold and windy day but our hearts were ignited with the warmth that the Truth of God's word brings when received with joy.

Half way down the track we noticed a garden with a sign above it reading "Gethsemane." Sharp bits of broken slate formed the floor of this garden and a carefully planted row fruit trees were visible as a border. Not quite the olive grove where Jesus went to pray with His disciples but none-the-less a place for quiet meditation for what was to come. We seemed to instinctively know we had to move forward so without words we walked on together. Taking time to listen and ponder upon the words on the signs and what God might be saying today through them. Eventually we arrived at the Cross.

Knowing we had to go alone across the bridge for our own personal encounter with God at the Cross, we waited for each other before setting off back to the farmhouse.

However, before our visit to the farm, I had felt prompted to pick up a small bottle of anointing oil I had bought whilst in Israel and God reminded me of this. Made conscious of the sacredness of the moment and differing nations represented at the Cross on this special day, I asked Joosun and Susan if they would like to return to the foot of the cross with me to pour oil at the base of the cross and to cry out to God that this Holy place may continue to be a place of healing and unity for future generations and the nations of Israel, South Korea and the United Kingdom.

At the tender age of 14 I remembered being impacted by a love like none other I had ever known as someone preached about the Cross and what Jesus had done by paying the price for the sin of all humanity. I felt dirty in the light of such purity and love and I knew I needed a Saviour so I simply said,

"Here I am Lord, if you love me enough to die for me I just want to live for you."

It is here a new adventure begins for at the moment of each letting go of the old there is potential for the new thing God has to do in and through each one of us when we say

"Here I am, wholly available."

This world may continue to try to fit you into its mould but let us cast ourselves at the feet of the Master Blacksmith for then we will be positioned in the right direction to herald and see His coming again.

Restoration is to do with "putting things back in the right place in their right condition." No one can do that but God when it comes to our lives and the world.

The Apostle Peter, filled with the Holy Spirit, preached to a crowd of people in Jerusalem in these words;-

"Repent, then, and turn to God,
so that your sins may be wiped out,
that times of refreshing may come from the Lord,
and that He may send the Christ,
who has been appointed for you – even Jesus.
He must remain in heaven until the time comes
for God to restore everything,
as he promised long ago through his holy prophets." [70]

Could it be that we are now in that time of "Restoration of all things?" albeit we have had to come through the fires of testing and trials to the place of cleansing and purifying.

---

70) Acts 4 v 18 – 21

As you have journeyed with me to The Forge are you ready for:-

Activation rather than vegetation

Surrender rather than Survival,

Faith rather than Fear

Are you ready to become undone

to see God's Kingdom Come?

The promise of God through the Prophet Joel was,

"I will restore to you the years that the swarming locust has eaten." [71]

This will be true now in your life as in mine for the times of restoration are here and the Kingdom of Heaven is at hand.

THE LORD IS COMING SOON!

---

71) Joel 25 v 1a

Printed in Great Britain
by Amazon